# BOOKS BY CAROLYN MEYER

## NON-FICTION

Amish People:
PLAIN LIVING IN A COMPLEX WORLD

Eskimos:
GROWING UP IN A CHANGING CULTURE

The Center:
FROM A TROUBLED PAST TO A NEW LIFE

*(Margaret K. McElderry Books)*

## FICTION

C.C. Poindexter

Eulalia's Island

The Summer I Learned About Life

The Luck of Texas McCoy

*(Margaret K. McElderry Books)*

# BOOKS BY CHARLES GALLENKAMP

Maya: THE RIDDLE AND REDISCOVERY OF A LOST CIVILIZATION
*(for adult readers)*

The Pueblo Indians in Story, Song and Dance

Finding Out About the Maya

The Mystery of the Ancient Maya

# THE
# MYSTERY
## OF THE
# ANCIENT
# MAYA

CAROLYN MEYER
AND
CHARLES GALLENKAMP

A Margaret K. McElderry Book

ATHENEUM 1985 NEW YORK

Unless otherwise noted, all photographs are by Charles Gallenkamp

LIBRARY OF CONGRESS CATALOGING IN PUBLICATION DATA

Meyer, Carolyn.
The mystery of the ancient Maya.
"A Margaret K. McElderry book."
Includes index.
Summary: Explores the advanced civilization and unsolved
mysteries of the Maya, who reigned for six centuries
and then disappeared.
1. Maya—Juvenile literature. [1. Maya.   2. Indians
of Central America]   I. Gallenkamp, Charles.   II. Title.
F1435.M56  1985     972.81'01     84-24209
ISBN 0-689-50319-9

Published simultaneously in Canada by McClelland & Stewart, Ltd.
Composition by Maryland Linotype Composition Company
Baltimore, Maryland
Printed and bound by Fairfield Graphics
Fairfield, Pennsylvania
First edition

# CONTENTS

# Contents

## Contents

PART
ONE

# ADVENTURES
# IN
# DISCOVERING
# A
# LOST
# CIVILIZATION

# CHAPTER

## I

# A
# TALE
# OF
# TWO
# TRAVELERS

Two travelers—one American, one English—struggled through the jungle, hacking away the tangled vines with their machetes. New York City, which they had left that fall of 1839, seemed impossibly far away. Since their arrival in Central America the trip had been grueling. In the past few weeks they had endured hunger and been thrown into a makeshift prison. They had hung on as their mules picked their way along the edges of cliffs. But now, standing on a river bank in Honduras, they felt hopeful again. On the opposite shore they could make out a stone wall, perhaps a hundred feet high but nearly hidden by the thick growth of trees. Maybe this was what they had been searching for— the lost city of Copan.

Quickly they forded the stream and climbed a weathered stone stairway they found that led to a terrace. From there the two men could distinguish the remains of other structures in the surrounding jungle. Then they slowly descended into the shadowy depths of the rain forest, into the midst of wonders far beyond anything they had dreamed of finding.

All around them were the remains of huge pyramids, stairways, platforms, buildings, and walls, shattered by the roots of trees and vines that grew in the cracked stones. Gigantic sculptured blocks of stone were scattered about, some still standing, some fallen over or broken, their surfaces carved with masks, animals, human figures, and strange symbols. A dense canopy of trees blotted out the sun. Except for the cries of exotic birds and the rustle of monkeys in the branches overhead, the gloomy forest was silent.

"All was mystery," John Lloyd Stephens wrote in his journal, describing the scene, "dark, impenetrable mystery."

Stephens, the American, and his companion, Frederick Catherwood, were jubilant as well as awestruck. They *had* found what they were looking for—Copan, the lost city.

They had heard rumors and stories; now here was proof, not only of a single lost city but, as it turned out, of an entire ancient civilization. And Copan was just the beginning. Over the next three years Stephens and Catherwood explored more than forty ruins in the jungles and highlands of Mexico and Central America. Many were to come after them, but they were the pioneers who wrote the first chapters of the fascinating story of the people we now know as the Maya. The civilization of these people had once rivaled the achievements of the ancient Egyptians and Greeks. But somehow, at some time, the Maya civilization had mysteriously vanished, leaving tantalizing clues but no explanations.

The two friends who made archeological history during their travels were an unlikely pair of explorers. John Lloyd Stephens, always the more famous of the two, was born in 1805 and grew up in New York City. John studied law as his father wished, and by the time he was nineteen he had a law degree. But John Lloyd Stephens

Portrait of John Lloyd Stephens, the nineteenth century explorer-author whose books first brought the ruined cities of the ancient Maya to wide public attention. (*Photo of a painting, taken by Stuart Rome; Courtesy of American Museum of Natural History*)

was a restless young man with a touch of wanderlust. For a while he traveled throughout the United States, eventually returning to New York and settling down to practice law. Over the next nine years he became deeply involved in politics and earned a reputation as a fine speechmaker. Then a doctor diagnosed a throat ailment and prescribed a long trip abroad. It was exactly what John Stephens wanted to hear.

Stephens was not an ordinary tourist, content with seeing the usual sights of London, Paris, and Rome. Having done that, he journeyed off the beaten path to places like Russia and Poland, sailed down the Nile to inspect the ruins of Egypt, and trekked across the desert to Arabia. But after two years of exotic travel, he went home again to his law practice.

One day Stephens learned from a conversation with someone in the publishing business that books about travel were extremely popular. Stephens decided that writing was much more interesting than practicing law; easier, too. He dashed off two volumes based on his experiences in Egypt, Russia, and Arabia, and the books became bestsellers of their day. That was all Stephens needed to lock the door of his law office for the last time and to start planning his next trip. It would be to some exotic region—the kind of place he knew people wanted to read about.

He picked Central America. Intrigued by early accounts of lost cities buried deep in the jungle, he studied everything he could about the area. There wasn't much. Most scholars at that time believed that prehistoric Americans had been nothing more than savages, incapable of creating anything of importance, and certainly not magnificent cities. The few accounts he was able to find—one by an officer in the Spanish army, for instance—indicated otherwise. John Lloyd Stephens made up his mind to see for himself.

Then Stephens met Frederick Catherwood, an English architect whose taste for travel to faraway places matched Stephens'. So did his talent: Catherwood's drawings of ruins in Egypt were well known. The two men—Stephens was then thirty-two, Catherwood six years older—immediately struck up a friendship. Stephens proposed that they go to Central America together, in search of the ancient ruins of Copan. Catherwood agreed. They began to get ready for their trip.

Stephens had political connections, and he used them to get himself appointed diplomatic agent to the Central American Confederation. There was no great competition for the job. For one thing, everyone who had held the position had died in office. For another, civil wars had flared up in the countries Stephens planned to visit. The whole area was infested with roving soldiers, bandits, and smugglers. However, the appointment entitled Stephens to a trunk full of impressive documents and an elegant coat decorated with rows of brass buttons. Stephens collected his documents and his coat, Catherwood bought a supply of paper, pens, and ink, and the two adventurers set sail from New York in October of 1839.

Stephens and "Mr. C," as the writer referred to the artist in his journals, arrived in what is now called Belize City and went on by steamer to a small village in Guatemala. They hired guides and pack mules to take them across the rugged mountains into the rain forest.

From the beginning the journey was dangerous. Slowly they climbed the mountain's treacherous slopes on muleback. At one point the steep path led through a gulley so narrow the animals could barely squeeze through, and Stephens was afraid he would have a leg crushed. Sometimes the mules stuck fast; sometimes they slipped in the mud and fell. Next they were surrounded by an impenetrable wall of jungle, dragged through mudholes, thrown against trees. In all his travels, Stephens had never endured anything like it. And this was just the beginning! As they pushed on it became harder and harder to imagine that any civilization ever flourished in such hostile surroundings.

The city of Copan in Honduras, as it appeared about A.D. 700. (Reconstruction drawing by Tatiana Proskouriakoff; *Courtesy of the University of Oklahoma Press*)

Eventually the way became easier, but scarcely had that danger decreased than another kind of peril threatened them. Just a few miles from their destination a ragged band of fierce men seized them and imprisoned them in an abandoned church. The next day they

were released without any explanation, and once again they were on their way, over the border into Honduras.

The village the Indians called Copan was a disappointment—half a dozen miserable thatched huts, ruled over by a bad-tempered tyrant named Don Gregorio. The unfriendly *don* made no secret of wanting to get rid of them, but he grudgingly directed them to an Indian guide who could lead them to the useless pile of stones they were determined to see.

The Archway at Labna in Yucatan as drawn in 1842 by Frederick Catherwood, the English artist who accompanied John Lloyd Stephens on his travels.

The ruins of the ancient city of Copan were anything but a disappointment. Welcome or not, they made up their minds to stay and explore their discovery.

Stephens wrote; Catherwood drew. For a while they made Don Gregorio's hacienda their headquarters and astonished the villagers with their strange habits, like brushing their teeth. There was so little space to hang their hammocks that they slept with their hips low and their feet as high as their heads. "Vexacious and ridiculous," Stephens complained and announced that they would sleep in the ruin. But there was no place to hang the hammocks, and it was wet and muddy under the dripping trees. The two ended up sharing the hut of a poor couple who, Stephens noted, lay with their heads at opposite ends of their bed of woven branches so that one could smoke without disturbing the other.

Meanwhile, the muleteer who had brought them this far turned as stubborn as his animals and refused to stay any longer. While the explorers pondered their next move, a newcomer, Don José María Acevedo, arrived on the scene and advised them that he was the owner of the "idols." He also mentioned that his wife was ill; he had heard that the two foreigners had medical skills. While Catherwood went off to the ruins to sketch, Stephens visited the wife. As a quasi-doctor, he diagnosed rheumatism, advised the patient to keep her feet dry, and promised to send some liniment for her aching neck. Now, he felt, he had earned her husband's gratitude and would be allowed to work at the ruins without interference.

"The only way to make a thorough exploration would be to cut down the whole forest and burn the trees," Stephens wrote, but that idea was impractical as well as undesirable. They decided to limit themselves to making careful measurements (Stephens' job) and drawings of the sculptured columns (Catherwood's).

Catherwood had the harder task. The carving was cut unusually deep into the stone, and the jungle light was so dim that Catherwood could not see well enough to sketch the intricate figures. They picked one of the stone sculptures and tried to cut down the trees around it, but here again were problems. There were no axes, only *machetes*—chopping knives—fine for clearing away shrubs and branches but practically useless on a large tree. Furthermore, Stephens observed, the Indians were not inspired workers. One would hack at a tree until he got tired of the job (which Stephens thought happened very quickly), and then another would take a few whacks. It was slow going, but at last a few trees were felled and Catherwood, with better light on his subject, began to draw.

Next Stephens hired two *mestizos* (people of mixed Indian and Spanish descent), offering them rewards for every new discovery. They could see only a few yards ahead, never knowing what they'd stumble on next. The two helpers went to work with their machetes, cutting away vines and branches, digging in the earth of the jungle floor to uncover a carved eye, an ear, a foot. The more they found, the more excited Stephens became. When their steel blades clanged against the stone, Stephens impatiently pushed the workers away and began to dig in the loose earth with his hands. "The beauty of the sculpture, the solemn stillness of the woods, disturbed only by the scrambling of monkeys and the chattering of parrots, the desolation of the city, and the mystery that hung over it"—all of this fascinated Stephens more than anything he had seen among the ruins of the Old World. Within a few hours he had returned to Catherwood to report more than fifty objects to be copied in drawings.

But Mr. C. was less than delighted with Stephens' report. His feet in a mud puddle and gloves on his hands to protect them from clouds of hungry mosquitoes, he gloomily contemplated his drawings. The designs on the sculptured columns were so complicated and the subjects so different from anything he had ever seen that Catherwood was having a hard time copying them. "The 'idol' seemed to defy his art;" Stephens wrote, "two monkeys on a tree on one side appeared to be laughing at him, and I felt discouraged and despondent."

But not daunted. They found some waterproof boots which "lifted Mr. Catherwood's drooping spirits, who was ill with a prospective attack of fever and ague or rheumatism, from standing all day in the mud." The next day, a more comfortable artist was also more successful. The light was right, and he had finally gotten the hang of it.

The Temple of the Magician at Uxmal, Yucatan. (*Drawing by Frederick Catherwood*)

Meanwhile difficulties loomed on other fronts. Don Gregorio still wanted to get rid of them. Rumors flew that suspicious foreigners found snooping around the ruins would be shot if certain political factions discovered them. The owners of the hut where they were

Stela H at Copan, Honduras, erected in A.D. 782. This drawing was made by Frederick Catherwood in 1839. Such monuments were carved by the Maya to commemorate events in the lives of their rulers, or to record calendrical dates and information of religious importance.

staying were afraid for the explorers' lives as well as for their own. To reassure them, Stephens delved into his trunk and produced his diplomatic credentials. But he and Catherwood also began carrying pistols.

When the political situation had settled down, Stephens got an idea: he would try to buy the ruins of Copan. He visited Don José María, the owner of the ruins, and offered him fifty dollars. "I think he was not more surprised than if I had asked to buy his poor old wife, our rheumatic patient, to practice medicine upon. He seemed to doubt which of us was out of his senses."

Don José María protested that he might get into trouble if he did business with a foreigner. Stephens once more flashed his impressive documents. But "the shade of suspicion still lingered; for a finale, I opened my trunk, and put on a diplomatic coat, with a profusion of large eagle buttons. I had on a Panama hat, soaked with rain and spotted with mud, a check shirt, white pantaloons, yellow up to the knees with mud . . . but Don José María could not withstand the buttons on my coat."

The transaction went through. "I paid fifty dollars for Copan," Stephens reported. "There was never any difficulty about the price. I offered that sum, for which Don José María thought me only a fool; if I had offered more, he would probably have considered me something worse."

In April of 1840, after Stephens and Catherwood had done as much as they could in Copan, they began a search for the ruins of Palenque in the Mexican state of Chiapas. It was a long, hard journey from Copan, and their main thought once they reached Palenque was to recover from their "shattered condition." Catherwood shook with malarial fever, and Stephens was weakened from the effects of exposure and insect bites. The excitement of discovering the ruins of Palenque drove them on, but the drenching rains and suffocating heat didn't let up. Snakes and reptiles, lizards and scorpions infested the ruins and tormented them. They slept little. By June they could stand it no longer and left Palenque, boarding a ship for Yucatan and the ancient city of Uxmal. But their stay in this beautiful ruin was cut short. Catherwood collapsed and became delirious. It was time to go home. They arrived in New York City at the end of July 1840.

Stephens immediately sat down to write a book about their adventures, and Catherwood finished a set of elegant engravings to illustrate it. *Incidents of Travel in Central America, Chiapas, and Yucatan*, in two volumes, appeared in June of 1841 and touched off a storm of controversy. Historians searched for ways to explain the evidence of the amazing civilization reported by Stephens and Catherwood.

While scholars argued, the indomitable pair prepared for a second expedition and left for Yucatan that fall. It took them six weeks to finish their survey of Uxmal, three months to investigate several other ruins. They camped at Chichen Itza, the most famous of Yucatan's archaeological sites, in March of 1842. Early in April they sailed to Cozumel Island to explore it and the city of Tulum on the nearby mainland. But after seven months in the field, Catherwood was again too sick to continue, and in May they left for home.

Early the next year Stephens' new book, *Incidents of Travel in Yucatan,* was published. It was a great success—his books are still widely read—but his adventures did not make him as rich as he had hoped. Catherwood was plagued by bad luck of various kinds. His drawings were a major part of the books, but he never got the recognition he deserved. The two remained friends but did not collaborate again. Frederick Catherwood's life ended in 1854 when his ship went down at sea on a crossing to New York from England. John Lloyd Stephens never returned to the land of the Maya. He died of malaria in 1852 at the age of forty-seven.

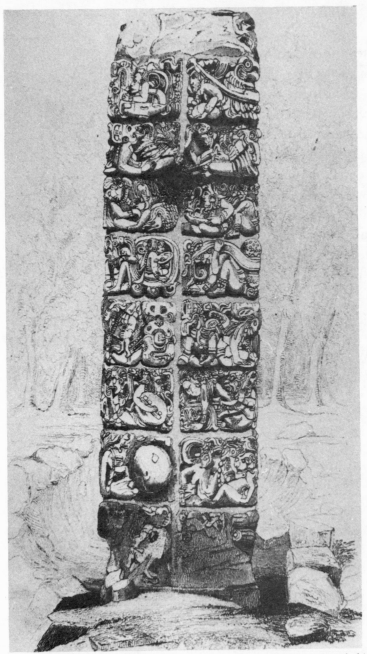

Stela D at Copan, Honduras showing a calendrical inscription as recorded in Maya hieroglyphs. (*Drawing by Frederick Catherwood*)

Stephens has been called "the father of Maya archaeology." He brought the splendors of Maya civilization to the world's attention. His explorations opened the way for scholars to begin examining these remarkable ruins systematically. This research has provided some of the answers to questions that had bothered Stephens from the first hectic days at Copan: How did these people transport the stone from the quarry those long distances through the jungle when the wheel was unknown to them? How did they carve those beautiful sculptures without metal tools? What did the symbols on the columns mean? Who were these people and what happened to them?

Stephens wrote, "Here were the remains of a cultivated, polished, and peculiar people, who had passed through all the stages incident to the rise and fall of nations, reached their golden age, and perished entirely unknown." When he asked the Indians of the area, "Who were these people?" the answer was always the same: "*Quién sabe?*" —"Who knows?"

Many of the mysteries have been unraveled. But many still remain.

CHAPTER

II

# DESTROYERS
# AND
# PRESERVERS

*Oro!* the Spanish seaman whispered. "Gold!"

His companions saw it, too. They didn't stop to discuss it; they just grabbed whatever ornaments they could get their hands on and ran.

The men had been on a slave hunt, in 1517, in the Caribbean, for Carib Indians, under the command of Francisco Hernández de Córdova. Their ships were blown off course by a storm, and they had landed on the northeastern tip of Yucatan, a thumb-shaped peninsula that projects into the Gulf of Mexico. They were hungry and thirsty, but they were also amazed by what they found—mysterious cities defended by hordes of fierce warriors who left the Spaniards' leader mortally wounded. In the midst of these cities stood beautiful temples where the seamen scooped up necklaces, small figures, and head-dresses made of copper and low-grade gold.

Those lucky enough to escape somehow made it back weeks later to Cuba, where they were based, wounded and sick but eager to tell their wild tales. And they had the loot as proof. Low-grade or not, the gold had aroused the Spaniards' greed.

On his last voyage in 1502, Columbus had encountered a canoe off the coast of Honduras carrying Indian traders from a province called *Maia* or *Maiam*. This was the first recorded contact with the people we call the Maya. But the outside world did not hear about these Indians until fifteen years later when the ragtag band of Spanish slave traders became the first white men to set foot in the Maya realm, a 125,000-square-mile area including Guatemala, Belize, and parts of Mexico, Honduras, and El Salvador, about the size of the state of New Mexico.

The next year the Spanish returned. Indian traders mentioned the fabulously rich Aztec empire in a region they called *Méjico*. The Spaniards pressed on "in the direction of the sunset" and were met by messengers sent by Montezuma, the Aztec emperor, bringing presents of gold. If Montezuma hoped the white men would be satisfied and go away, he was wrong. The gifts simply whet their appetites for more, and more was never enough. In search of gold, the adventurers stumbled instead upon two of the most highly advanced native civilizations ever known in America: the Aztecs of Mexico and the Maya.

The famous Spanish *conquistador*, Hernando Cortés, and his troops invaded the Aztec kingdom in 1519 with horses and guns—neither of which the Indians had seen before—and thousands of Indian allies who hated the lordly Aztecs. Within two years Cortés had defeated their once-powerful armies, destroyed their magnificent capital, Tenochtitlan, and made off with a fortune in gold, silver, and precious stones. And he opened the way for a tide of conquest and colonization to sweep through the rest of Mexico and Central America.

In 1523 Cortés sent one of his captains with an army of Spanish soldiers and Indian allies to conquer Guatemala and El Salvador. Three years later another Spanish adventurer, Francisco de Montejo, launched a more difficult campaign to defeat the Maya of Yucatan. That attempt was a failure, but in 1541 Montejo's son resumed his father's war. With a well-equipped army, the conquistadors crushed the Indian resistance. By the end of 1546 the Spanish controlled most of Yucatan, except for the jungles of northern Guatemala. (It would be another century and a half before the stubborn Maya in that area were conquered.)

The Maya were reduced to a miserable life of persecution and poverty. The land was taken away from them and handed over to colonists who came from Spain to settle in the New World. The colonists were entitled to the services of the Indians to whom the land had once belonged; in return, the new owners were supposed to protect the Indians. Instead they exploited them, and when the Indians resisted, the rebels were severely punished or sold into slavery. Although attempts were made by some churchmen to abolish slavery and to help the Indians, the landowners protested. Laws were made to satisfy them.

Even more harmful to the Maya were the diseases carried by the Europeans. The Maya had no natural immunity against smallpox, influenza, measles, tuberculosis, or amoebic dysentery. When these illnesses struck, the populations of some villages were reduced by three-quarters, some by as much as nine-tenths.

The first conquistadors were awed by what they found in the vast wilderness—ornate palaces, pyramids crowned with temples, elaborate courtyards, and paved roadways. Chieftains in jaguar-skin robes and headdresses of bright feathers came out to greet them, and priests performed strange rituals to honor their gods in temples smoky with incense. For the Spanish soldiers the goal was gold, but for the Christian missionaries who came after them, the goal was *God*. The Franciscan and Dominican friars, trained in the zeal of the Spanish

Inquisition, believed they were called to convert the idol-worshipping Indians to the Christian faith.

Ferdinand and Isabella, the King and Queen of Spain, had established the Spanish Inquisition in 1478. Its purpose was to find and punish converts from other religions who were not thought to be sincere Christians. Soon not only former Jews and Muslims were being persecuted; any Spaniard—even those who had always been Christians—could be arrested, brought to trial on trumped-up charges, tortured, and sentenced to death. It happened all the time.

Out of this harsh tradition came the missionaries sent to Yucatan. Some churchmen did try to protect the Indians against abuses by the government and the church, but so-called Christian ideas were more often ruthlessly enforced by brutal means. Whipping, beating, mutilating, and scalding were part of a long list of inventive methods of torture employed by many followers of the gentle-spirited St. Francis.

One of the most ambitious and fanatical of these missionaries was a young Franciscan friar, Diego de Landa, who arrived with a boatload of monks in 1549 to live in a monastery near the town of Merida. Landa vowed to stamp out every sign of the Indians' religion. He saw to it that native shrines and idols were destroyed wherever he found them. His dedication paid off. Within twelve years Landa was made head of the Franciscan order in Yucatan.

Not long after that, one of his assistants found evidence of pagan worship and sacrifice in the town of Mani, about forty miles from Merida. Landa ordered a mass imprisonment of the villagers and had many of them, both men and women, tortured. Several died while their tormentors tried to make them confess; others were permanently mutilated. As a climax, on July 12, 1562, Landa staged an auto-da-fé, a burning (the word means "act of the faith"). Into the huge bonfire went idols and idol-worshippers alike—and a number of codices, books filled with Maya hieroglyphic writing.

A codex, or book, was made of strips of paper eight or nine inches

Diego de Landa, the Bishop of Yucatan and author of the *Relación de las Cosas de Yucatán*, a detailed account of Maya culture and traditions which has given archaeologists one of their most valuable sources of information. (Photo of a painting, reproduced by permission of the Peabody Museum of Archaeology and Ethnology, Harvard University)

wide and several yards long. The strips were from the bark of the wild fig tree, strengthened with a natural gum, and coated with smooth white stucco, a mixture of powdered lime and water. On this surface scribes drew figures and symbols and colored them with vegetable and mineral paints. The strip was then folded back and forth like a fan to form pages.

Scholars believe that the codices Landa burned may have held a key to Maya hieroglyphics—picture-writing—that could have allowed them to decipher the meaning of the symbols carved on many of the temples and columns and stairways. Knowledge of Maya literature, history, and science—all believed to have been included in these codices—might have survived. Then we would have a clearer answer to the question asked by Stephens and Catherwood and many who came after them: "Who were these people?"

But it was too late. The books were destroyed. "We found a great number of books in these characters," Landa wrote with satisfaction, "and, as they contained nothing in which there was not to be seen superstition and lies of the devil, we burned them all, which they regretted to an amazing degree and caused them affliction."

The Bishop of Yucatan, who had been away in Mexico City at the time if the auto-da-fé, was furious when he returned and found out what had happened. He released the prisoners and packed Landa off to Spain to be dealt with by the Council of the Indies. Landa and his accomplices, the angry bishop wrote to the Spanish king, were men of "little learning and even less charity."

Landa found himself in trouble when he arrived in Spain in 1563 and was ordered to account for his actions. Either to defend himself or to provide a guide for young missionaries—nobody knows which—he wrote down everything he knew about the Maya. And it turned out that he knew a great deal about the people he had treated so harshly. Soon after his arrival in Yucatan fourteen years before, he had begun a thorough study of Maya culture to prepare himself for his missionary work. He became fluent in their language, Yucatec. He spent time with members of the families that had once been the region's most powerful rulers, questioning them about every aspect of native life. He gathered information from local Indians whenever he had the chance. In the process, he had become an expert on the culture he was trying to abolish. Now he wrote down his observations

Bishop Landa's famous "alphabet," an early attempt to translate Maya hieroglyphic writing in which Landa recorded hieroglyphic symbols that, when pronounced in the Yucatecan language, corresponded to letters of the Spanish alphabet. For example, the first figure shows the head of a turtle; since the Yucatecan word for turtle was "ac," Landa mistakenly equated it with the letter "a." (Reprinted from *Relación de las Cosas de Yucatán* by Diego de Landa, edited by A. M. Tozzer; courtesy of the Peabody Museum of Archaeology and Ethnology, Harvard University)

in a manuscript called *Relación de las Cosas de Yucatán* (*History of the Things of Yucatan*).

Landa ultimately triumphed. He was cleared of the accusations against him. After the old bishop died, Landa was sent back to Merida in 1573 as no less than the new Bishop of Yucatan. And he immediately resumed his former practices of persecuting the Indians in the name of Christianity, all the while observing their culture, until his death a few years later. Then, for nearly three hundred years, his

Detail of Maya hieroglyphs found on a carved tablet at Palenque, Chiapas.

manuscript dropped from view. No one gave the *Relación* another thought.

His friends considered Abbé Brasseur de Bourbourg charming and witty, if perhaps a bit odd. This nineteenth-century priest had some truly outlandish notions, but he also had an unusual knack for turning up rare manuscripts. One day in a library in Madrid he came across a heap of papers, fragile and crumbling with age: it was a copy of Landa's long-lost manuscript. Parts of the manuscript were missing, but most important sections were there. Brasseur's discovery in the 1860s opened a new chapter in the study of the Maya.

The Abbé Brasseur could not have been more different from his Franciscan brother, Landa, of three centuries before. Abbé Brasseur had both the "learning and charity" that Landa lacked. He also had a reputation as a student of antiquities and as a lover of Maya culture. Unlike Landa, Brasseur was no fanatic about anything but his ancient manuscripts. He sometimes said that he would never have had access to priceless private collections if he had not been a good Catholic.

Brasseur made several trips to America, but without the advantage of adequate financial backing he often had to sell whatever he owned in order to continue his travels. He was a strikingly attractive and intelligent man, and his winning personality helped him to meet and earn the trust of people who could assist him. He had a great gift for languages—he spoke twelve fluently and could read another twenty.

But Brasseur was also an incurable romantic, given to embracing wild theories based on flimsy evidence. At a time when most scholars still believed that the sophisticated culture of Central America had its roots in Egypt, Brasseur insisted that it was just the other way around! Sometimes he argued that the Maya were descended from Scandinavian ancestors—or Phoenician, or Hindu, or inhabitants of the mythical continent of Atlantis. His arguments were inconsistent, in the extreme.

Only three Maya codices are known still to exist. The authenticity of a fourth discovered in 1971 is still debated. One of the first people to attempt a translation of the strange pebble-shaped characters in one of these hieroglyphic books was Abbé Brasseur. It was a long and discouraging task; sometimes he was not even sure if the hieroglyphs were in the Maya language. But eventually he was positive he had cracked the code, and he published his two-volume translation in

A page from the
Dresden Codex, the
finest of the surviving
examples of Maya
codices or books.
(*Courtesy of the
University Museum,
University of
Pennsylvania*)

French—before it was discovered that he had read all of the characters *backward*. Cyrus Thomas was the scholar who, in 1882, defined the order in which the glyphs are read, left to right and top to bottom.

Foolish as some of his notions may have been, Brasseur was a talented collector, managing to unearth documents that others overlooked. Rummaging through a second-hand bookstall in Mexico City, he found an old manuscript that he bought for four pesos. It turned out to be the only known copy of a Maya-Spanish dictionary complied by a Franciscan friar about 1580. But his most important discovery was Landa's manuscript. *Relación de las Cosas de Yucatán* is by far the best account of ancient Yucatan written during the colonial period. Rich in details of folklore and religious beliefs, rituals and ceremonies, history and the arts, social customs and daily life, the *Relación* is considered vital to understanding the Maya and is still widely used by archaeologists. But no one ever quite understood Bishop Landa, a paradox who remains one of the most fascinating and dismaying of the destroyers/preservers of Maya civilization.

Of the three native manuscripts similar to those burned by Bishop Landa that have survived, one turned up in Vienna in 1739 and was later acquired by the Royal Library in Dresden, Germany. Another— the one Brasseur "translated"—was found in Spain during the late nineteenth century, and the third was discovered in 1860 in a box of old documents in a library in Paris. No one knows how they got to Europe, but probably they were taken there by Spanish soldiers as souvenirs or gifts. All three deal with astronomy, prophecy, and calendar rituals, and not with historical events or daily life.

A series of books written by Indians who learned Spanish from the missionaries tell a great deal about Maya history in the centuries just before the Spanish Conquest. The *Books of Chilam Balam* describe the history and folklore of Yucatan before the Spanish arrived. A manuscript from Guatemala known as the *Popul Vuh* records mythology, traditions, and history of the Maya who once dominated the southern highlands. But these manuscripts do not shed any light on what happened during the zenith of Maya civilization. It took a long succession of explorers and scientists to accomplish that.

# CHAPTER
## III

# THE LAST
# OF THE
# ROMANTICS

They begged him not to do it, but Edward Herbert Thompson wouldn't listen.

He had read about the Well of Sacrifice in Bishop Landa's book. "Beautiful maidens and captive warriors of renown, as well as rich treasures," Landa had written, "were thrown into the dark waters of the Sacred Well to propitiate the angry god who, it was believed, lived in the deeps of the pool." Now Thompson was determined to explore the well and prove the truth of the legend. Even if it killed him.

Sinkholes, called *cenotes*, where the limestone surface has collapsed to expose underground rivers, are found throughout Yucatan. One of them at the ancient city of Chichen Itza was used as a water reservoir; the other was a sacred ritual and devotional center. This unattractive water hole measured about one hundred and sixty-five feet across and two hundred feet long. Limestone walls towered some seventy feet above the surface of the murky water, green with algae. Beneath forty feet of water lay another forty feet of mud and silt. The cenote fascinated Thompson. "From the moment I read [Landa's] musty old volume, the thought of that grim old water pit and the wonderful objects that lay concealed within its depths became an obsession to me."

But when he presented his idea for going down into the dark waters of the Sacred Well to his friends, they were horrified. "If you want to commit suicide," they asked him, "why not seek a less shocking way of doing it?"

About the time the scholarly Abbé Brasseur de Bourbourg was poking around old manuscripts in a library in Madrid, a small boy named Edward Herbert Thompson was poking around in the fields near his home in Massachusetts, hunting for Indian arrowheads. Later, as a teenager, Edward Thompson read John Lloyd Stephens' books and was fired with *Mayismo*—enthusiasm for the Maya culture. That flame never died. While he was in college (studying first business and then engineering, neither of which he really wanted as a career) Thompson read a book by Brasseur that convinced him the Greek legend of Atlantis was based on fact. He wrote an article titled "Atlantis Not A Myth," claiming the Maya were a branch of the lost civilization of Atlantis, a continent that supposedly sank in the Atlantic Ocean.

The article did not establish Edward's reputation as a scientific thinker. But his Mayismo attracted the attention of some wealthy and influential men looking for a person to carry out archaeological investigations in Yucatan. The benefactors chose Thompson and arranged to have him appointed United States consul for Yucatan and Campeche, two Mexican states in the Yucatan Peninsula. He was to devote his free time to research. His sponsors gave him broad guidelines: investigate the ancient Maya ruins and the modern Maya people. Within those limits, he could do whatever he wanted.

Edward invested a few intense months teaching himself what he thought he would need to know. He learned something about medicine, to be able to take care of himself and his wife. He read up on psychology, in order to deal with the natives, and learned to handle a gun (in case psychology didn't always work). He mastered photography and studied Spanish, although he preferred to learn the Mayan language directly from the Maya. He read whatever he could find about the people he was going to study. And then in 1885, barely twenty-five years old, he left for Merida, the capital of Yucatan.

Edward Thompson lived in Yucatan more than forty years, twenty-

Edward Herbert Thompson, the archaeologist who explored the Well of Sacrifice at Chichen Itza. (Reproduced from *City of the Sacred Well* by T. A. Willard)

33

The Well of Sacrifice, Chichen Itza. Note the small temple at edge (foreground) from which sacrificial victims were thrown into the water.

four of them in the dual role of public official and private explorer. One of his early projects was to make molds of the exterior walls of some of the important structures. He concocted a mixture of paper pulp, native fibers, and plaster, and put the Indians to work on this huge project. The work went well at the site in Labna, but the climate in Uxmal, only a few miles away, made everyone sick. Thompson went temporarily blind from his illness. Still, he managed to finish the job and got the molds shipped off to Chicago for the 1893 World's Fair.

Thompson did his most important work at Chichen Itza, one of the greatest centers of Maya civilization. When he arrived there, many of the ruins were only shapeless heaps of stone. But with the backing of a wealthy Chicagoan who sailed to Yucatan on his yacht, Thompson bought the estate on which the ruins were located and began to restore the hacienda. He made it habitable and moved his family there from Merida, eighty miles away. He imported cattle and planted corn, hiring people to tend the estate, with the idea of earning enough from the sale of farm products to support a scientific center for scholars. Thompson was a dreamer, and although some of his dreams came true, that one did not.

A kind and simple man, he liked the Maya and they liked him. He learned their language, and they appreciated his interest in their ancient customs. They trusted him so much that they took him into their secret brotherhood organization. He was the first white man permitted not only to watch their yearly dance drama in traditional masks and robes, but to film and record the symbolic ceremony. But, typically, he pursued what interested him and ignored the rest. And so he learned little about Maya mythology and religion, in spite of his relationship with the brotherhood, and he made few attempts to interpret the carved figures on the buildings.

While he was exploring Chichen Itza, Thompson came upon two large, polished stones imbedded in what had once been the floor of a temple on top of a pyramid. Beneath these stones he discovered a shaft going down about twelve feet into the core of the pyramid. At the bottom of the shaft he found the remains of a skeleton and some broken pottery bowls—and beneath this four more graves, one on top of the other.

This wasn't the end. Under the lowest grave he found a stairway going down into a chamber. But the stairwell was filled with ashes, and the only way he could get to the chamber was to lie on his back and push feet first through the ashes. Inch by inch he worked his way into the narrow vault. A stone slab rested against one wall. When Thompson tried to move it, the slab gave way, uncovering a great black hole in the floor beneath it. A cold blast of air from the cavern blew out the candles and left Thompson and his Maya assistants in the dark. Thompson later described the scene.

"Don Eduardo," his workmen cried, "this is surely the mouth of Hell!"

"Not so," he soothed them. "Since when has the mouth of Hell given forth a breath as cold as this wind?"

His answer convinced them, at least for the moment.

The circular opening was about three feet across. Thompson let down a lantern attached to a rope and estimated the depth at about fifty feet. Then he had two men hold his ankles and lower him head first into the hole to take a look. At dawn the next day, a knife clamped between his teeth, pockets stuffed with tools, Thompson went down by rope into the darkness.

By the light of his lantern, he gazed at the first of many treasures, an alabaster vase filled with polished jade beads and a beautiful pendant. His assistants scrambled down the rope to join him in what is now called the Tomb of the High Priest. All day long they worked, discovering one exciting relic after another. It was eleven o'clock that night when they decided to quit and go up to the outer world. There they found the families of the workmen weeping and wailing, positive that the Great Serpent had taken them all away, while Thompson's wife tried to reassure them.

Thompson recorded this as "one of the red-letter days in my life as an archaeologist." There were more red-letter days ahead (as well as many black ones). Thompson's biggest and most dangerous adventure was the exploration of the Well of Sacrifice.

Bishop Landa himself had peered down at this evil-looking pool and written about the terrible secrets he had learned from his Indian informants: "Into this well they . . . had the custom of throwing men alive as a sacrifice to the gods, in times of drought, and they believed that they did not die though they never saw them again. They also threw into it a great many other things, like precious stones and things which they prized. And so if this country had possessed gold, it would be this well that would have the largest part of it, so great was the devotion which the Indians showed for it."

Most scholars dismissed Landa's statement as legend, but Thompson believed that legends were rooted in truth. This one fired his imagination, and he began to devise a plan to search the waters of the cenote for remains of ancient sacrifices made by the Maya to their gods.

Thompson took his time plotting and scheming. He returned to the United States and assembled all the equipment he needed and had it crated, ready for shipment. While he was in Boston, he took deep sea diving lessons. Then when everything was ready he went to his sponsors and presented his idea for exploration of the Sacred Well. They didn't like the idea at all. They were sure something terrible would happen to him, and they didn't want to be responsible. But Thompson was not easily put off; eventually he talked them into giving him the moral and financial support he needed.

In February of 1904 he set up a dredge and derrick next to the Well of Sacrifice, and with the help of thirty natives he went to work. At first he was discouraged. "The dredge bucket went up and down interminably it seemed, bringing up loads of rock, punk and muck, and depositing on the observation platform rock, punk and muck only," he wrote. "I began to get nervous and sleepless of nights."

After a week of unproductive dredging, the bucket brought up a ball of yellow resin called *pom*, sacred incense, which had been thrown into the well as part of the offerings mentioned in traditions. Thompson was overjoyed. "That night I slept long and well."

From then on each dredge load of slimy mud held new evidence of the truth of the legend. Out of the murky water they lifted a myriad of items made by Maya craftsmen: pottery, jade figurines, beads, pendants, objects of copper and gold—only a low-grade alloy, but richly carved. In addition to all this, up came human bones and skulls, the remains of sacrificial victims thrown into the well as Landa had reported. The dredging continued, until the bucket began to come up empty again.

Then Thompson decided it was time to take the ultimate risk. He would dive into the pit himself.

Thompson donned his diving gear: a suit of waterproof canvas, a big copper helmet that weighed more than thirty pounds, with plate glass goggle eyes, and iron-soled canvas shoes. Speaking tubes, air hoses, and life lines were sorted out and he prepared to descend, accompanied by two Greek sponge fishermen. The natives, who had been working with Thompson for years, came to shake his hand. "They were bidding me a last farewell, never expecting to see me again. . . . I sank like a bag of lead, leaving behind me a silvery chain of bubbles."

The water was thick with mud, the consistency of pea soup, and no light could penetrate it. Thompson had to get used to doing everything by feel and to the sensation of weightlessness. Rocks dropped on them from overhead, and rising too quickly to the surface on one occasion permanently damaged his ears. But the hazards of working in such dangerous conditions paid off. They found pottery, carved jades, copper bells, golden bowls, fragments of fabric, spear throwers, and sacrificial knives. Many of the objects may have been deliberately broken, "killed" so that their spirits could escape.

There were bones, too, not of "beautiful maidens and captive warriors of renown," but of many children under twelve as well as adult men and women—all sacrificed to appease the gods who dwelled beneath the dark water.

A far different kind of trouble lay ahead for Thompson than anything he or his worried friends had anticipated. In 1921, during a period of civil unrest, when he ordered some of his tenants to pay the back rent they owed him, they burned his house at Chichen Itza, destroying his library and collection of artifacts. Then in 1926 Thompson announced his exploration of the Sacred Well and the precious objects that he had been shipping off for two decades to the Peabody Museum in Boston for study. The Mexican government promptly confiscated his estate at Chichen Itza on the charge that he had stolen national treasures.

Not long after that Edward Thompson left his beloved Yucatan where he had lived and worked for forty years. Poor and sick, but proud of his accomplishments, Thompson died in 1935 at the age of seventy-nine. He had been one of the foremost contributors to Maya research, but the professional archaeologists who came after him ignored his work or ridiculed it. They were a new breed of explorers whose Mayismo was scientific, and Thompson had been, after all, a romantic.

# CHAPTER

## IV

# THE
# BEGINNINGS
# OF A
# MYSTERIOUS CIVILIZATION

The shots were fired without warning, and several men, including the physician for the group, fell dead. If the leader of the expedition had not been too nearsighted to ride at the head of his men, he would have surely been killed by the Guatemalan soldiers who ambushed the archaeologists, mistaking them for revolutionaries. But Sylvanus Morley survived the "hierglyphic hunt" at Uaxactun, one of the most ancient of Maya cities, and once more brought back some exciting new discoveries.

In 1912 at Copan he had been lashed to a mule and taken on a three-day ride out of the jungle, delirious with malaria. Another time he had nearly died from amoebic dysentery. Then in 1916, sponsored by the Carnegie Institution, he was field director of the expedition to Uaxactun. Despite all the hardships, he considered this the most successful of his "hunts" in the jungles of Yucatan—even after trigger-happy government troops started shooting.

"May 5th—Friday [1916]," he had scribbled in his journal a few days before the attack. "A remarkable day, all things considered. At about eight o'clock six of us . . . left for the ruins. An hour and a half in a southerly direction brought us to the champas of San Leandro, where we left our horses and proceeded the rest of the way on foot. We filled our canvas buckets at the aguada and started off in a westerly direction . . . and in half an hour we were skirting the right hand edge of a small ravine, on the edge of which the ruin stands."

One of the party had sighted a *stela*, a monument with carved inscriptions, but Morley was disappointed; most of the glyphs had been worn away. Then a shout announced the discovery of another monument. Morley could read its date, and his mood changed. "Black disappointment instanter gave way to complete satisfaction. All those weary leagues, those heated arguments, those 'multitudinous humbugs' had not counted for naught." For the next few days, Morley and his companions labored to raise fallen stones and to copy their dated inscriptions.

"Only liars and damn fools like the jungle," Morley grumbled, but that never kept him from putting up with its miseries. Year after year he searched for hieroglyphics on stelae and monuments that would help to unravel the mystery of the Maya.

Edward Thompson had been a loner, going his own way, following his own inclinations. Stephens and Catherwood were an eccentric pair. The Abbé Brasseur de Bourbourg was a hopeless dreamer. All of them were talented and dedicated, but not one was a scientist. Morley was as obsessed with the Maya as any of them had been, but he was a new kind of explorer: a scientist trained in archaeology.

A word derived from Greek meaning "the study of beginnings," archaeology is defined by the modern world as the study of the life and culture of ancient peoples. Research into the distant past began in the fifteenth century, when Italian scholars with some knowledge of ancient Greece began to excavate Greek sculpture. Interest in antiquities spread next to Egypt. In 1799 Napoleon's troops discovered a stone slab, named the Rosetta Stone for the town in which it was found, inscribed in both Greek characters and Egyptian hieroglyphics. Twenty-two years later, a French scholar named Champollion used the Rosetta Stone to decipher the Egyptian symbols. Then attention shifted to the archaeology of the Middle East. But until Stephens and Catherwood came along in the nineteenth century, the cultures of the Americas were almost completely ignored.

The study of the Maya has become a much more complicated undertaking than it was in the days when Edward Thompson put on a diving suit and jumped into the Well of Sacrifice. Present-day archaeology involves highly technical methods of locating, excavating, interpreting, recording, preserving, and sometimes restoring evidence of past cultures. This requires the skilled assistance of a long list of experts: historians, anthropologists, linguists, geologists, chemists, physicists, botanists, architects, engineers, photographers, climatologists. All of them are searching in different ways for answers to the same questions: Who were these people? What happened to them?

A hundred years ago few people believed that civilizations as advanced as the Maya and other New World cultures could have been indigenous—that is, originating in the areas in which they lived. Their roots had to lie somewhere else. No one knew where, but there were plenty of theories: Europe, Asia, the Near East, and Africa were all suggested. Many people thought that the American Indians were descendants of the Lost Tribes of Israel, referred to in the Bible.

In the nineteenth century the Nile Valley was suggested as the source, and there did seem to be certain similarities between the civilizations of Egypt and the Maya area. Both had built pyramids, temples, and elaborate tombs; both developed low-relief sculpture and hieroglyphic writing; both worshiped the sun. Maybe, scholars theorized, early inhabitants of the western hemisphere had been visited by Egyptians, traveling either by ship or by some vanished land connection.

Or maybe the Maya were survivors of a "lost continent" long since submerged beneath the sea. There were stories of one such continent sunk in the Indian Ocean, a second in the Pacific; the third and most famous—Atlantis—supposedly lay on the bottom of the ocean just west of the Straits of Gibraltar.

Atlantis was the creation of the Greek philosopher Plato, who described an imaginary paradise where Atlanteans lived carefree lives until they became corrupt and their angry gods plunged their beautiful island to the ocean floor. Plato had invented his story to prove a philosophical point, but many people forgot that it was fiction. Abbé Brasseur de Bourbourg, who was fond of wildly romantic notions, once insisted that Atlantis had been the source of all ancient civilizations, including those of Mexico and Central America. And lots of people—including, for a time, Edward Herbert Thompson—agreed with him.

For years the debate raged on. New theories came and went, all trying to prove that America's aboriginal cultures were either founded or strongly influenced by immigrants from distant lands.

But John Lloyd Stephens insisted that the ruins he explored belonged to a culture originating right there. "The works of these people," he wrote, "are different from the works of any other known people; they are of a new order ... they stand alone." For a long time Stephens' idea was considered revolutionary. Even when Edward Herbert Thompson arrived in Yucatan more than forty years later, he followed Abbé Brasseur de Bourbourg's thinking. But after only a year in the field Thompson too was convinced that the Maya culture did indeed stand alone.

It was an Englishman named Alfred P. Maudslay who turned Maya research into a science. Beginning in 1883 Maudslay made nu-

Alfred P. Maudslay camped at Chichen Itza in 1889. Maudslay's explorations helped usher in the birth of scientific archaeology in the Maya area, and his early photographs of ruined structures and monuments are among the finest ever taken. (*Photograph by H. N. Sweet*)

merous expeditions throughout Yucatan, southern Mexico, Guatemala, and Honduras. (Thompson worked with him for a short time.) He mapped and excavated undiscovered sites and surveyed buildings. He made plaster casts of monuments and inscriptions, later shipped to the Victoria and Albert Museum in London, and took hundreds of photographs of Maya antiquities. He collected folklore from the local Indians. His five-volume work on the archaeology of the area set a high standard of scholarship.

Meanwhile various scientific institutions had joined the field of Maya research and sent their experts to begin systematic excavations of the ruins. Deposits beneath the ruins were excavated over a wide area and the contents of each layer examined. By classifying the pottery fragments they found and tracing stylistic changes in art and architecture, they were able to piece together the stages of cultural development.

Developed in 1947, a technique called radiocarbon dating has helped to pinpoint accurately the length of time involved in that process. Radiocarbon dating is an ingenious method of determining the age of organic matter. It is based on the presence of a radioactive substance known as carbon 14, which accumulates within all living plants and animals. When the organism dies, the carbon 14 begins to disintegrate gradually at a fixed rate. Measuring the amount of radioactive carbon in a fragment of organic material (such as bones and teeth, wood, antlers, ivory, hoofs, seashells, and fiber) indicates the span of time from the date of the death of the animal, or the date when the tree or plant was cut down, until the present. For instance, sections of the wooden door lintels at Tikal have been studied by this method. A small amount was burned and the carbon 14 measured, indicating when the trees the lintels were made from had been cut. Then this information was checked against the inscriptions carved on them.

One of the awesome tasks confronting Maya scholars has been to decipher Maya hieroglyphics. Epigraphers like Sylvanus Morley who studied ancient inscriptions realized that the Maya system of writing was unique, totally unrelated to other kinds of writing. No other Indian culture had a true written language. The Aztecs used a kind of picture writing, and the Incas of Peru invented *quipus*, knotted strings with which they kept amazingly complex records. But neither of these was anything like the writing of the Maya.

The closest thing scholars had to a "Rosetta Stone" was Bishop Landa's *Relación*, in which he tried to translate Maya glyphs into the Latin alphabet. This was only partly successful, because he didn't realize that a single glyph might represent a complete word or idea as well as a phonetic sound. But Landa did come up with an explanation of how the calendar worked and made drawings of the hieroglyphics representing the days and months with their Yucatec names.

At Copan the Hieroglyphic Stairway has sixty-two steps, thirty-three feet wide, constructed with over two thousand individual stones, each carved with a glyph. This is the longest known Maya inscription. Several large panels with hundreds of glyphs were found at Palenque, and the entire back of a pyramid-temple at Tikal is covered with hieroglyphics. Dozens of monuments, altars, and pottery vessels have been found with hieroglyphics. For a long time the code seemed unbreakable, but computer technology has helped to crack parts of it. Only a portion of the symbols dealing with history, religion, or mythology have been interpreted, but most of the inscriptions about the calendar, astronomy, and mathematics can now be easily read.

Scientists have learned a lot about the Maya so far, but the list of unanswered questions seems endless. Big questions, like exactly where Maya civilization originated, how it developed where it did, or exactly why it all ended, are still debated. Smaller questions, like details of social organization and daily life, are still puzzles. Answers come slowly, but they come.

The first humans arrived in America from Asia across the Bering Strait sometime between twenty thousand and forty thousand years ago and slowly spread throughout most of this hemisphere. They carried flint-tipped spears, dressed in animal-skin clothing, and knew how to make fire and use stone tools. They found shelter in caves and hunted large animals now extinct. They were the direct ancestors of the American Indians.

By about 7000 B.C. many of the animals on which these ancient hunters had depended for food were becoming scarce. People began to gather seeds, roots, and nuts to add to the small game they killed. About six thousand years ago these first Americans learned to cultivate the plant called maize, or corn, possibly first in the highlands of Guatemala or central Mexico. People began to move around less and to live together in one place.

Remains of peoples who were definitely ancestors of the Maya date from about 2000 B.C., and the earliest pottery (one of the indicators of settled village life) found so far in the Maya area comes from a site in Belize. A linguistics expert analyzed the Mayan language and came to the conclusion that some groups of Mayan-speaking people had also settled in northwestern Guatemala about 2600 B.C.

Scientists have been able to sketch only the roughest outlines of what life was like during the early centuries of this distant epoch, known as the Preclassic period. Families lived together in clusters of one-room huts made of poles lashed together with vines and plastered with mud, a style that has scarcely changed at all. Special buildings for religious ceremonies were set apart from these huts. Temples or shrines that looked a lot like the peasants' homes were erected on flat-topped pyramids. Little by little religious architecture developed a style of its own and became more elaborate and highly decorated. Important temples built around open courtyards formed ceremonial areas near the center of each settlement.

As time passed, these settlements grew into thriving cities. On the outskirts the Preclassic Maya planted crops, gathered wild fruits and vegetables, and hunted small game. Distinctive clay figurines were often found at their settlements, female forms three to six inches high with wide hips, narrow shoulders, and tiny heads. They were probably fertility symbols.

The Maya developed in the southern part of an area called Mesoamerica, the name given to those areas of Mexico and Central America where pre-Columbian cultures like the Aztec and Maya developed. That part of Mesoamerica included two separate environments. The highlands were blessed with rich natural resources and a pleasant climate. The lowlands on the other hand were extremely hot, humid, insect-ridden, and jungle-covered—generally a miserable place in which to live. Historians have had to reexamine the "rule" that sophisticated civilizations could not flourish in an environment as inhospitable as the lowlands seemed to be, because it was precisely in that area that Maya civilization reached its greatest heights.

Like other primitive people, the Maya began to make gods of the sun, the rain, and many other aspects of nature that they saw were essential to their survival. They knew that life depended upon having the right amount of sun and rain to supply food for the growing population. As more deities were invented to deal with life, pleasing all of them became more complicated. An endless round of ceremonies required specialists—priests—who knew how to perform them. It was the priests who practiced hieroglyphic writing, the priests who understood the complicated calendar, the priests who demanded the building of elaborate temples. Naturally they became extremely powerful. Religion was the driving force behind the development of Maya culture, and the priests gave the orders.

The Maya were obsessed with the passage of time. Wanting to mark its passing in some visible way, they erected stelae carved with a date to commemorate an important historical or religious event or to mark the end of a specific time period. The oldest Maya inscription found so far in the lowlands is on a stela at Tikal in Guatemala with a date that corresponds to July 6, A.D. 292. By the time that stela was put up, Maya civilization was entering its most glorious stage—the Classic period. For the next six centuries the Maya would display their remarkable brilliance in art, architecture, mathematics, astronomy, and writing, and then fade like a comet that streaked across the tropical sky.

PART
TWO


UNEARTHING THE EVIDENCE:
SIX
CENTURIES
OF
BRILLIANCE
COMES
TO
LIGHT

# CHAPTER

## V

# THE
# SECRETS
# OF A
# TOMB

Alberto Ruz Lhuillier stared at the flagstone floor of the Temple of Inscriptions, high atop a terraced pyramid at the ancient city of Palenque. There was something peculiar about it. Near the center of the room lay an unusually large stone with circular holes drilled around its edges, all filled with plugs to conceal them. No one had been able to figure out what they were for—and the site had been studied intensively since Stephens and Catherwood had stopped there more than a century before. But Ruz, an archaeologist from the Center for Maya Studies in Mexico, noticed something other explorers had missed: the walls of the temple seemed to continue on below the floor, as though another room lay beneath it. On a hunch, Ruz decided to raise the stone.

As workmen struggled to lift the heavy slab, Ruz could make out the outlines of a narrow opening completely filled with large stones and clay. There was nothing to do but haul out this debris. After a few days of digging, a series of stone steps began to appear, an interior staircase leading down into the pyramid. Ruz resolved to follow the stairway to its end, even though he knew it would involve an enormous amount of labor.

For two and a half months Ruz and his men struggled against heat, humidity, and choking dust while they hauled up the heavy rocks with ropes and pulleys. It took them four such stretches—a total of ten months—to clear the staircase. By the end of the first season, in the summer of 1949, only twenty-three steps had been uncovered. At the end of the third season they had dug out sixty-six steps and were down about seventy-three feet beneath the temple floor, near ground level. They still had no idea where the stairway was leading and no clues to its original function. No inscriptions were visible on the walls, no sculpture had been found. But at the bottom of the stairs they did find a box of offerings—pottery dishes, jade beads, jade earplugs, and a beautiful tear-shaped pearl. They knew they were getting close.

During the summer of 1952 the diggers encountered a wall. "The wall turned out to be more than twelve feet thick;" Ruz wrote, "breaking through it took a full week of the hardest labor of the entire expedition. The mortar held so firmly that the stones often broke before they separated, and the wet lime burned and cracked the workmen's hands. Finally we got through and came upon a rude masonry box or chest."

Inside the box were six human skeletons, at least one of them female. "Unquestionably this was a human sacrifice," Ruz wrote, "young persons whose spirits were forever to guard and attend him for whom all this entire massive pyramid had been made—and whom we now soon hoped to find."

Excitement mounted. Next they discovered a low triangular doorway sealed by an enormous stone, and they managed to loosen it enough for Ruz to squeeze behind it and into a vaulted room. He

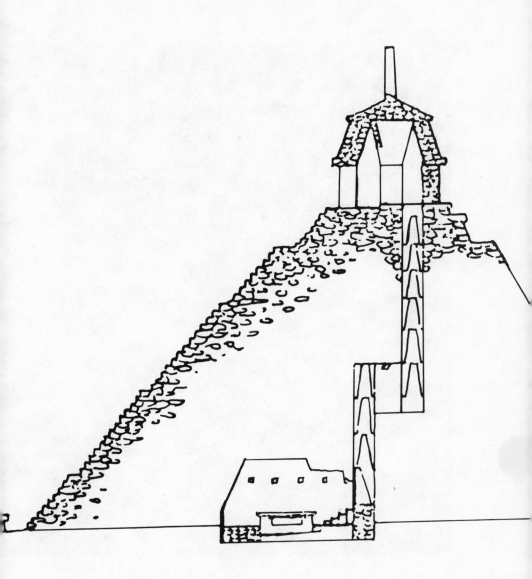

A cross-section of the Temple of the Inscriptions at Palenque, showing the location of the stairway and burial vault discovered by Alberto Ruz in 1952. (*Redrawn from a drawing by John Skolle*)

The Great Palace, Palenque. One of the most extraordinary buildings ever
erected by the Maya, this Classic-period structure contains a series of
inner courtyards, corridors, rooms, and subterranean chambers built on an
artificial platform.

knew instantly that his four seasons of exhausting labor had been rewarded.

"Out of the dim shadows emerged a vision from a fairytale, a fantastic, ethereal sight from another world. . . . Across the walls marched stucco figures in low relief. Then my eyes sought the floor.

This was almost entirely filled with a great carved stone slab, in perfect condition. . . . Ours were the first eyes that had gazed on it in more than a thousand years!"

The chamber was about twenty-nine feet long by thirteen feet wide, the steeply vaulted ceiling twenty-three feet high. Human figures modeled in stucco relief, probably representing the gods of the underworld, paraded around the walls. A colossal monument filled up most of the room: a beautifully carved stone slab resting on another immense stone which in turn was supported by six huge chiseled blocks.

Ruz believed that he had found a ceremonial burial place, but he would have to wait to find out. It was mid-July; the rains had come, and funds for that phase of the exploration were gone. Ruz had to leave Palenque and his exciting project until November.

When he returned, Ruz had a narrow hole drilled into the base stone, and when the bit reached a hollow space he poked a wire through the opening. The particles of red paint that stuck to the wire told him this was not an altar but an incredible coffin. But to prove this he would have to lift the sculptured stone slab, weighing about five tons and a masterpiece of Maya art. Ruz spent two days getting ready. Hardwood logs cut in the forest were brought to the pyramid and lowered by cables through the interior staircase. Then jacks were placed under the corners of the slab, reinforced by the logs.

"On November 27, at dusk, after a twelve hour working day, the soul-shaking manoeuvre took place." Inch by inch they raised the slab. Ruz saw that a cavity had been carved in the huge base stone, and the cavity was sealed with another polished stone, also fitted with plugs. When the slab had been lifted up about fifteen inches, Ruz could stand the suspense no longer. He squeezed under it, removed the plugs from the inner cover, and peered in.

Green jade ornaments, red-painted teeth and bones, the fragments of a mask—Ruz gazed at the remains of the man for whom all of this

Interior of the burial vault in the Temple of the Inscriptions, showing the gigantic carved slab that covered the sarcophagus containing the skeleton of a lord named Pacal, who ruled Palenque from A.D. 615 to 683. (*Courtesy of the Instituto Nacional de Antropología e Historia, Mexico*)

A jade mosaic mask that covered the face of Pacal. This magnificent mask was part of a lavish offering of jade ornaments placed in the grave, and it represents a superb example of the skill with which the Maya worked jade— a mineral highly prized for its beauty and ritual importance. (*Courtesy of the National Museum of Anthropology, Mexico*)

had been created. A treasure of jade ornaments had been placed on the dead man at the time of his burial—headdress, earplugs, bead collar, breastplate, rings on every finger, bracelets, and sandal beads. A single jade bead had been placed in his mouth to make sure that the spirit of this king or high priest could buy food in the afterlife.

The body had been wrapped in a cotton shroud painted red and sprinkled with powdered cinnabar, a red mineral. A magnificent mask made of jade mosaic with shell and obsidian inlays for the eyes had been fitted over the face of the corpse. The mask is so lifelike that it was probably an actual portrait made while the noble was still alive.

For years before the dignitary died, the whole community had helped to prepare the tomb. After his death the body was carried down the stairway to the crypt, probably accompanied by a procession of priests in elaborate ceremonial dress, and laid in the stone coffin, the inside of which had been painted red, the color of death. Then they closed the coffin and moved the massive carved slab into place. Jewels were placed on the slab and some clay containers with food and drink were left behind, along with two beautiful heads modeled in stucco. The crypt was sealed by sliding the stone block into position in the narrow entrance. Then the six young people were killed—maybe sons and daughters of important nobles—to accompany and serve the dead man in the next world. Through a stone duct that Ruz found, which ran along the wall of the stairway all the way to the floor of the temple, the priests could communicate with the spirit of the dead man below.

Ruz's discovery yielded an enormous amount of information about this civilization. The complicated structure of the temple proves the skill of Maya architects. The carved slab over the stone coffin and the two stucco heads place Maya sculptors among the world's finest. The magnificent jade ornaments demonstrate their talent as craftsmen.

Stucco sculpture depicting the head of a young maize god. From the burial vault of Pacal in the Temple of Inscriptions, Palenque. (*Courtesy of the National Museum of Anthropology, Mexico*)

The Temple of the Sun, Palenque. Note the use of the openwork "roof comb" on the top, a decorative device found on many Maya temples, which was intended to increase the illusion of height.

Palenque, perhaps the most beautiful of Maya ruins, represents the peak of Maya achievement during the Classic period. It also shows the huge amount of effort that could be summoned from engineers, artists, stonemasons, and laborers, and the lengths to which the Maya people would go to honor a priest-king.

The Maya glorified their gods and honored their rulers through art and architecture. The temples that dominated Maya cities were designed to be awesomely dramatic. Maya architects used various techniques to achieve this effect, usually building temples on pyramids or platforms and adding elaborate stone crests called roof combs to make them seem taller. They decorated the upper faces of the buildings with sculpture in cut stone or stucco—a kind of plaster made of lime—and they painted them bright colors.

In contrast to the outside splendor, the rooms inside their buildings were small, dark, and damp. A few had openings for ventilation, but usually doorways let in the only light and air. Sometimes the walls were brightened with murals, but mostly they were plain white stucco.

Although they weren't laid out according to any formal plan, cities were used for religious ceremonies and government activities as well as for the rulers' residences. The higher the family's status, the closer it lived to the center of town: priests and nobles near the temple, professionals and wealthy merchants further out, and the peasants on the fringes. In some cities groups of buildings and monuments were arranged to serve as astronomical observatories. Sweat baths were common—rooms with stone benches, drainage troughs, and hearths for boiling water. They designed artificial reservoirs to catch the rain and underground bottle-shaped pits called *chultunes* to store water and food. (Edward Thompson had himself lowered by rope, knife clenched between his teeth, candle in one hand, into more than a hundred of these dank caves to determine what they were used for.)

A panel of three elite figures in characteristic poses. The man on the left
clearly shows the effects of artificial skull deformation, a trait highly desired by
the Maya, who flattened the foreheads of infants by binding them to boards.
This group was uncovered in a courtyard in the Great Palace at Palenque.

*Above:* A polychrome ceramic vase embellished with paintings showing an elite figure seated on a throne covered with a jaguar skin. From the Peten area of northern Guatemala. (*Courtesy of the Dumbarton Oaks Research Library and Collection, Washington, D.C.*)

*Right:* A ceramic vase from Altar de Sacrificios in Guatemala. The figure represents a dancer clad in a jaguar-skin headdress, gloves, and pants. Hieroglyphic inscriptions are painted on the rim and sides of the vessel, a common feature of Late Classic-period ceramics. (*Photo by Stuart Rome; courtesy of the National Museum of Archaeology, Guatemala*)

Almost every city had at least one ball court for a popular game known as *pok-a-tok*. About the size of a basketball court, it had sloping or vertical walls with a stone ring jutting out midway along each wall, just above the players' heads. The object of the game was to knock a solid rubber ball through the stone ring. The ball could not

be thrown or kicked—it had to bounce off heavily padded hips, shoulders, or forearms.

Two teams competed, skilled players were much admired, and scoring was rare. Bets ran high—jade, gold, houses, and slaves were wagered—and the winning team was allowed to collect the jewelry and clothing of the spectators—if they could be caught. Naturally everyone vanished as soon as the match was decided. Certain religious rites were connected with the game, which the Maya believed was a favorite sport of the gods. A series of low-relief sculptures in a ball court at Chichen Itza, showing players being beheaded, leads some scholars to say the losers lost literally everything.

Maya engineers designed elaborate drainage systems, aquaducts and bridges, roads and causeways. From twelve to thirty-two feet wide and raised several feet above the ground (higher in swampy areas), the "white roads", called *sacbeob* in Yucatec, were constructed of a smooth layer of cement over a base of stones. They linked important groups of buildings within cities, and some joined city centers to out-lying districts. The longest sacbe found so far runs sixty-two miles. The peasants walked along these roads, but when the nobility traveled any distance they did so in litters or large baskets carried on the shoulders of servants or warriors.

New cities were being founded all over the Maya realm, and older ones were continually being enlarged and improved. By A.D. 600 Tikal had become the largest city, with a population estimated as high as fifty thousand. Six pyramid-temples vary in height from 155 to

Detail of a carved stela from Yaxchilan, Chiapas. It shows an elite figure holding a scepter—a symbol of rank and authority. He is richly dressed in a *quetzal*-feather headdress, an elaborate loincloth or *ex*, ornate sandals, and jade ornaments. Such figures, common in Maya art, attest to the wealth and exalted position of the ruling class. (*Courtesy of the National Museum of Anthropology, Mexico*)

The Court Ball at Copan, Honduras, showing the game known as *pok-a-tok* being played with a rubber ball. (*Reconstruction drawing by Tatiana Proskouriakoff; courtesy of the University of Oklahoma Press*)

288 feet from ground level to rooftop. Beyond this central cluster, ruins of smaller temples and palaces extend for five miles. Copan, the intellectual center, had a main temple complex covering seventy-five acres, with other ruins extending for several miles beyond.

The labor required to build these cities was enormous. Thousands of peasants cleared and leveled the land and quarried tons of stone, dragging it to the site on log rollers. Hundreds of masons cut and shaped the stones and set them in place. The pyramids and platforms on which temples were built began with a central core of rocks and earth secured with retaining walls. (Unlike the pyramids of Egypt and a few exceptions, such as Ruz's discovery at Palenque, Maya pyramids were not built solely as tombs.) Although most of the temples and palaces were made of stone, the Maya never completely stopped using simple thatched huts for some of their religious buildings.

Maya feats of engineering are even more amazing considering that they did it all without wheeled vehicles or draft animals and without metal tools. They managed to erect huge, complicated buildings relying totally on manpower, stone tools, log rollers, and henequen fiber rope to help lift heavy objects.

The lack of the wheel throughout Mesoamerica has puzzled scholars for a long time. There is proof that the wheel and axle were known in the region: toy animals on wheels have been excavated in several parts of Mexico. But there is no evidence that the wheel was ever used for any practical purpose anywhere in the New World before the arrival of Europeans. Even the potter's wheel, introduced in the Old World over four thousand years ago, did not exist in Mesoamerica. Some experts argue that the *idea* of the wheel may have existed, but its circular shape had such important religious significance that it could not be adapted to practical uses. A more likely explanation is that there were no draft animals to pull a wheeled vehicle, and so there was no cause to invent the wheel.

The Maya never perfected the true arch, in which the space between walls is spanned with a curve of stones held in place by a wedge-shaped keystone. That type of arch had been in use in Europe since the sixth century B.C. Instead they devised the corbeled arch;

the stones are overlapped, each course or layer extending further out from the vertical wall than the course below it to form a triangular opening with a flat capstone at the top.

Sculptors shaped their materials with stone tools and possibly wooden mallets. When limestone is first cut, it is relatively soft and can be worked easily until it hardens after exposure to the atmosphere. Pieces of limestone were burned to powder over a wood fire. The powder was then mixed with water to make mortar for holding the

A ceramic figurine from the island of Jaina, Campeche; it depicts a ball player wearing a protective yoke around his waist and carrying what appears to be a helmet. (*Photograph by Stuart Rome; courtesy of the National Museum of Anthropology, Mexico*)

masonry in place and plaster for smoothing over the rough stone walls and for surfacing roads.

The Maya excelled in carving and polishing jade, mined from

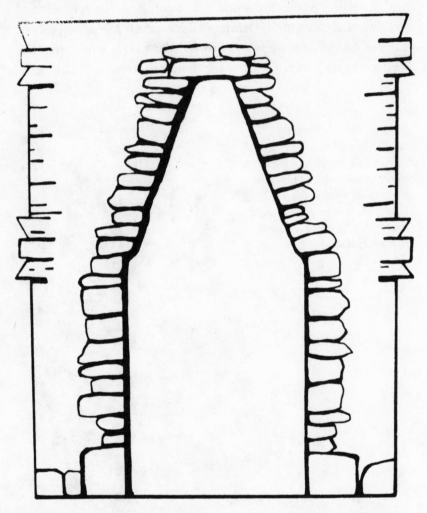

The Maya corbeled arch, showing a capstone at the top and the use of heavy stones set into the walls to provide support for the sides (*Drawing by Dolona Roberts*)

quarries in Guatemala, and occasionally picked up in streams. Varying from dark green to light blue green and even gray, it was prized for its beauty as well as its ritual uses. Tombs of important people, like those discovered by Thompson and Ruz, always contained lots of this mineral. Engraved, carved, or left plain, it was used in jewelry, figurines, and mosaics, and as inlays in stone and shell. Wealthy people liked to have bits of jade inset in their front teeth as a mark of social prestige.

The Maya were also excellent woodcarvers; a number of superbly carved wooden door lintels have been found at Tikal and in other places. They worked with bone, shells, and feathers, and created intricate mosaics and inlays with a few simple tools. There seemed to be no limits to Maya imagination and creativity.

From earliest times Maya artists were concerned with religious ideas. They used abstract symbols, but they also illustrated realistic scenes of religious rituals, human sacrifice, warfare, and daily life. Their sculptors produced powerful images of gods and mythical creatures, and of elegant human figures representing ruling lords or priests. These figures, generally shown in profile but sometimes facing straight forward with the head in profile, were dressed in elaborate costumes and jewelry, attended by servants, seated on thrones, or carried in litters. The artists lavished attention on detail, filling the spaces between the figures with hieroglyphics or decorative designs.

The Maya were master potters who produced all kinds of beautifully decorated forms, such as bowls, plates, vases, and jars, some with legs and removable lids. Sometimes they painted elaborate scenes on the pottery, called polychrome ware because it was decorated with several colors. Few examples of weaving and leatherwork, basketry, lacquered gourds, or work in other perishable materials have survived the effects of time, but the gorgeous costumes and headdresses pictured in sculpture and paintings show that they were skilled in these crafts too.

Metals weren't important to the Maya until after the Classic period ended around A.D. 900. They began to import copper and gold from other parts of Central America to use for ornaments and religious items. The greatest number of gold objects found so far were brought up from the infamous Sacred Well at Chichen Itza by Edward Thompson.

But in spite of all that investment of time, energy, and resources in their art, there are few images of common people—the laborers who built the cities, the farmers who produced food for an entire population, or the artists who portrayed the ideals of Maya civilization. Brilliant and ingenious as these creations are, the aloof figures frozen in stone seem remote and impersonal, leaving an impression of impenetrable mystery.

CHAPTER

VI

# AWESOME GODS, POWERFUL PRIESTS, AND BLOODY SACRIFICES

Bishop Landa was horrified, and who can blame him? He had heard more than he cared to about the Maya and their bloody human sacrifices, and yet he wrote down every detail, just as his Indian informants described them, just as he himself had seen them portrayed in the murals at Chichen Itza.

The victim was stripped and his body painted blue, the color of sacrifice. Then he was led to the top of a pyramid to a stone altar, curved so that, when he lay on his back, his chest was pushed upward. Four old men known as *chacs*, also painted blue, "seized the poor man whom they were going to sacrifice and with great haste, placed him on his back upon that stone and all four held him by the legs and arms so that they divided him in the middle."

Landa continued the grisly description. "At this time the executioner, the *nacom*, with a knife of stone, and with much skill and cruelty struck him with the knife between the ribs of his left side under the nipple, and at once plunged his hand in there and seized the heart like a raging tiger, tearing it out alive, and having placed it on a plate, he gave it to the priest, who went quickly and anointed the face of the idols with that fresh blood."

The gory ceremony continued as the corpse was hurled down the temple steps to another priest who skinned it, wrapped himself in the skin, and solemnly danced in it. The spectators completed the ritual by eating the rest of the body, saving the hands and feet for the officiating priests. By the time the ceremony was over, nearly everyone was smeared with blood, and the hair of the priests looked like clotted mops.

Sometimes victims were hanged or drowned, mutilated, disemboweled, beheaded, or beaten to death. And then there was a ritual known as the "arrow sacrifice." Landa described it this way.

"If he was to be sacrificed by arrows they stripped him naked and anointed his body with a blue color, and put a pointed cap on his head. When they had reached the victim, all of them, armed with bows and arrows, made a solemn dance with him around the stake, and while dancing they put him up on it and bound him to it, all of them keeping on dancing and looking at him. The foul priest in vestments went up and wounded the victim in the parts of shame, whether it were a man or woman, and drew blood and came down and anointed the face of the idol with it. And making a certain sign to the dancers, as they passed rapidly before [the prisoner] still dancing, they began one after another to shoot at his heart, which had been marked beforehand with a white sign. And in this manner they made his whole chest one point like a hedgehog of arrows."

Sacrifices at the Sacred Well at Chichen Itza were carried out differently; survival was possible. According to an early account, the priests and main participants spent sixty days in abstinence and fasting. At daybreak they came to the cenote and threw in their victims, instructing them to ask the gods who lived under the water for

78

A priest cutting out the heart of a sacrificial victim, Temple of the Jaguars, Chichen Itza. (*Drawing by Dolona Roberts*)

favors. Any victims who managed to stay alive until noon were hauled out by ropes, fires were built around them, and copal incense was burned. Then the survivors reported on what the gods had told them.

Sacrifices had always played an important part in Maya ritual. Animals and birds were sometimes offered, but the greatest sacrifice was the life of a human being. The Maya believed that human blood was essential to please the gods when the needs of the people were great, especially in time of drought. Although this gruesome practice was carried out during the Classic period, it became more common after A.D. 900, when it was intensified by invading Mexican groups who influenced the Maya. Victims were usually slaves, captured enemy soldiers, criminals, or orphans. Children, often preferred because of their innocence, were sometimes kidnapped or even purchased from neighboring cities. The usual price for a child-victim was from five to ten red beans.

The cruelty of these forms of worship are obvious. But while the Maya did not hesitate to sacrifice human life when they thought it was necessary, they never practiced it as the Aztecs did in central Mexico, often putting to death thousands of people at one time and waging wars in order to capture fresh supplies of victims.

\* \* \*

A bewildering assortment of gods ruled the lives of the Maya and inspired their marvelous accomplishments as well as their bloody sacrifices. Hunab Ku, the supreme being and creator of the universe, was so sacred that he never got involved in people's everyday lives. Itzamna, who may have been a manifestation of Hunab Ku, or perhaps his son, was usually considered "top god," the creator of human-kind. Sometimes he's shown as a toothless old man; other times he

Maya gods as shown in the hieroglyphic codices or books: (a) Itzamna, the creator god; (b) Yam Kax, the maize god; (c) Chac, the rain god; (d) Ah Puch, the god of death. (*Drawings by Dolona Roberts*)

looks like a reptile. A god with intellectual leanings, Itzamna was regarded as the inventor of books and writing and the patron of science and learning.

Ix Chel, the goddess of childbirth, weaving, and the moon, wore a headdress of entangled snakes and jewelry made of bones. Instead of toenails she had the claws of a jaguar. Chac, with his swooping nose and fangs, was in charge of rainmaking. He also had thunder, lightning, and storms under his control. To the Maya peasant who depended on Chac to water his fields, the rain god was all-important. Yam Kax, the young corn god, wore a headdress representing the maize plant. Ah Puch, the "Lord of Death," was always pictured with skeletal nose and jaw, fleshless spine, and spotted, decaying body. There was a god for merchants and travelers who also ruled the North Star. Important gods called *bacabs* determined which years were lucky and which were not. Bacabs were also the patrons of beekeeping. Virtually every activity the Maya could think of—hunting, fishing, and farming, war and trade, poetry and music—as well as suicide and human sacrifice, the earth and the sky, the calendar and numbers had their specific gods.

Most of these gods could be both friendly and unfriendly toward humans, sometimes being kind, sometimes angry, usually unpredictable. Itzamna was always benevolent, but the revered goddess, Ix Chel, had a dark side. She was responsible for sending floods, even though she protected women in childbirth and was the patroness of weaving and medicine. Some gods changed their physical characteristics and roles from day to night. And to make matters even more complicated, most gods had four identities, similar to the Christian idea of God as Father, Son, and Holy Spirit.

In the Maya way of thinking, the world was a flat, square surface that rested on the back of a gigantic crocodile floating in a lily pond. Above it thirteen "Upper Worlds" floated in layers and nine "Underworlds" were suspended beneath—all with their own gods. At the center of the earth grew a huge tree with a smaller tree at each corner. North, south, east, and west, each had a particular color, white, yellow, red, and black, and a bird of the matching color nested in each of the four trees with a specific god for each direction and color. The Maya believed that the earth had been created and destroyed several times in the past and that it would be destroyed again.

Ordinary people could hardly begin to know about all of these gods, to understand them, or to know how to please them. This was the role of the priests, who were properly trained and could intercede with the gods on behalf of the people. The highest category of priest was the *ahuacan*, whose duties included training younger priests in all the subjects they had to master—magic, ritual, science, and prophecy. Helping them were *chilans* or prophets, who studied the almanacs and interpreted omens in order to foretell the future. Nacoms and chacs (named for the rain god), assisted in the sacrifices. Shamans, called *ahmen*, devoted themselves to prayer and cures for illness.

Usually sons of older priests were chosen for the priesthood. Young girls from noble families could join religious groups of women who cared for the temples and tended the sacred fires that burned inside them. The girls could leave the group at any time, but boys who entered the priesthood faced a long and rigorous period of training.

Not only did the common people have scarcely any idea of what all this was about, but usually they were not even allowed to enter important temples and shrines. They may have taken part only in ceremonies that had to do with farming, hunting, fertility, and childbirth—matters that immediately affected their lives. During these rites peasants crowded into the cities to worship their gods and to enjoy the festivities. The complicated Maya calendar listed plenty of occasions for ceremonies, festivals, and banquets, many of them colorful affairs with gorgeous costumes and bright banners and streamers.

Masked actors and clowns performed plays, storytellers recited fables and legends, and musicians made music.

Most ceremonies started after a period of fasting (especially doing without meat, chili peppers, and salt) and sexual abstinence. After the purification rites came prayers, chanting, and ritual dancing. There may have been more than a thousand different dances, and the men and women almost always performed separately.

Burning incense was part of every ritual; pom, a resin of the copal tree, sent up clouds of heavy black smoke and filled the air with a fragrant odor. Sacrifices of food, ornaments, animals, pom molded in the shape of a heart and painted blue, and sometimes humans were an important part of worship. So was bloodletting; the participants stuck thorns or stingray spines through their ears, nostrils, lips, tongue, and other parts of the body and smeared the blood on the idols. The ceremonies usually ended with feasting and drinking *balche*, an intoxicating beverage made from maize—often too much balche. Sometimes the nobles' wives waited outside the banquets to help their drunken husbands to get home.

Bishop Landa raised his eyebrows at many of the goings-on in Maya cities, but especially at the drinking. "They made wineskins of themselves," he wrote sadly, "and this was the inevitable conclusion."

Like primitive people everywhere, the Maya peasants were overwhelmed by the mysteries of the universe around them and the planet on which they lived: the coming of the seasons, hard-to-predict phenomena like storms and eclipses, the human cycles of birth, reproduction, work, death—all seemed proof of the powers of the gods who controlled their lives and of their own powerlessness. They struggled against fear of the unknown, which has haunted humankind since the dawn of history. And like other people, they dealt with their fear through their religious beliefs, performing the rituals and accepting the authority of their priests who guided them through the never-ending and universal cycles of life.

# CHAPTER

# VII

# INTELLECTUAL
# GIANTS

he greatest race that ever lived on this earth,"
Sylvanus Morley insisted of his beloved Maya.
"The Greeks of the New World," he announced, boasting that their
calendar and discoveries in astronomy were "the highest intellectual
achievement" of any civilization existing in America before the coming of the Spanish.

There's no question of their intellectual brilliance.

The Maya were obsessed with the passing of time. Their method
of keeping track of time was more accurate than any calendar ever
used in the ancient world. Time to them was never simply a means
of recording events in some kind of order. It was a supernatural
phenomenon controlled by the gods, some of whom were good,
some bad. Each god was associated with a specific number and was
represented by a particular glyph in the inscriptions. (The Maya were
time-keepers but apparently not clock-watchers; there is no evidence

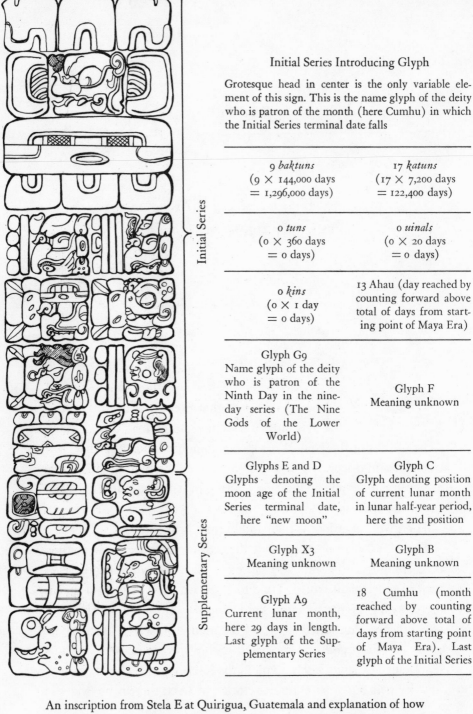

**Initial Series Introducing Glyph**

Grotesque head in center is the only variable element of this sign. This is the name glyph of the deity who is patron of the month (here Cumhu) in which the Initial Series terminal date falls

| | |
|---|---|
| 9 *baktuns* (9 × 144,000 days = 1,296,000 days) | 17 *katuns* (17 × 7,200 days = 122,400 days) |
| 0 *tuns* (0 × 360 days = 0 days) | 0 *uinals* (0 × 20 days = 0 days) |
| 0 *kins* (0 × 1 day = 0 days) | 13 Ahau (day reached by counting forward above total of days from starting point of Maya Era) |
| Glyph G9 Name glyph of the deity who is patron of the Ninth Day in the nine-day series (The Nine Gods of the Lower World) | Glyph F Meaning unknown |
| Glyphs E and D Glyphs denoting the moon age of the Initial Series terminal date, here "new moon" | Glyph C Glyph denoting position of current lunar month in lunar half-year period, here the 2nd position |
| Glyph X3 Meaning unknown | Glyph B Meaning unknown |
| Glyph A9 Current lunar month, here 29 days in length. Last glyph of the Supplementary Series | 18 Cumhu (month reached by counting forward above total of days from starting point of Maya Era). Last glyph of the Initial Series |

*Initial Series*

*Supplementary Series*

An inscription from Stela E at Quirigua, Guatemala and explanation of how a date is read. This inscription in the Maya Long Count calendar corresponds to January 22, A.D. 771. (Reprinted from *The Ancient Maya* by Sylvanus G. Morley, 3rd ed., revised by George E. Brainerd, with the permission of the Stanford University Press. Copyright © 1946, 1947, 1956 by the Board of Trustees of Leland Stanford Junior University)

that they divided the day into anything like hours or minutes, and so we assume that the day was the smallest unit of time they measured.)

The Maya had several ways of defining a year. The two hundred and sixty-day sacred year, called the *tzolkin* or "count of days," determined the pattern of ceremonial life for everyone. A baby's birthday was the day of the tzolkin on which it was born, and the god of that day was the baby's patron saint. The sacred year was not divided into months. Each day was assigned both a number from one to thirteen and one of the twenty Maya day names, which worked out to two hundred and sixty possible combinations.

The *haab* or civil year, sometimes called the "vague year," had three hundred and sixty-five days divided into eighteen months of twenty days each and an extra five-day month. The civil year was used for everyday affairs.

Meshing the three-hundred-and-sixty-five-day haab with the two-hundred-and-sixty-day tzolkin, like two interlocking cogwheels, produced the Calendar Round, with a total of 18,980 combinations and therefore 18,980 unique dates. That figures out to fifty-two years of three hundred and sixty-five days each from the start of one Calendar Round until the series of 18,980 began to repeat. (The Calendar Round did not belong exclusively to the Maya. It was widely used throughout Mesoamerica for recording time and foretelling future events.)

The Long Count, also called the Initial Series, is probably the most accurate calendar ever devised by an ancient civilization. It allowed the Maya to keep track of enormous spans of time. The Long Count consisted of nine recurring cycles, and the basic unit was the day or *kin*.

|  |  |
|---|---|
| 20 *kins* | equaled 1 *uinal* (20 days) |
| 18 *uinals* | equaled 1 *tun* (360 days) |
| 20 *tuns* | equaled 1 *katun* (7,200 days) |

20 *katuns* equaled 1 *baktun* (144,000 days)

20 *baktuns* equaled 1 *pictun* (2,880,000 days)

... And so on in multiples of twenty through *pictuns, calabtuns, kinchultuns,* and *alautuns* (the last of more than twenty-three billion days). Practically every Long Count inscription included only the first five of these, from *kins* through *baktuns,* and included the day of the Calendar Round on which the date ended. The Maya inscribed hieroglyphs in double rows of vertical columns, starting with baktuns at the top and ending with kins at the bottom. Archaeologists developed a shorthand for writing dates translated from the hieroglyphics. For example, *9.12.8.14.1  12 Imex  4 Pop* stands for 9 baktuns, 12 katuns, 8 tuns, 14 uinals, and 1 kin, ending on a Calendar Round date when 12 Imex of the sacred year meshes with 4 Pop of the civil year. The date is A.D. 681, found on a sculpture in Piedras Negras, Guatemala.

One big challenge scholars faced was figuring out the starting point of the Maya calendar, a date that functions like the birth of Christ, from which we count forward and backward in our system. Then they discovered that every Long Count inscription was calculated from a "zero date" of 13.0.0.0.0  4 Ahau  8 Cumku, corresponding to 3114 B.C. Because this date actually occurred over three thousand years before the earliest known Maya inscription, Sylvanus Morley suggested that it is not an actual date, but probably the date on which the Maya believed their world had been created or their gods came into existence.

Matching the Maya calendar with ours was still another problem. Counting backward from known events was one way, but the Maya system had changed by the sixteenth century and complicated that approach. The development of carbon 14 dating finally verified what is known as the Goodman-Martinez-Thompson system. The "GMT correlation," as it is also called, is now universally accepted (until something better comes along).

Diagram showing how the Calendar Round operated, the meshing of the 260-day almanac or *tzolkin* with the 365-day year. (Reprinted from *The Rise and Fall of Maya Civilization* by J. Eric S. Thompson, 2nd edition, Copyright © 1966, with the permission of the University of Oklahoma Press)

Each unit of the Maya calendar—kins, uinals, tuns, and longer cycles—was pictured as a "burden" carried on the back of one of the gods assigned to it. At the end of each unit the burden was set down by the god that had been carrying it and picked up by the god of the next number according to the calendar. Suppose that at the end of the day called 6 Zip the god of the number 6 puts down his burden, the month of Zip. Immediately the god of the number 7 picks up Zip, carries it on his back for twenty-four hours, and then passes it on

| Pop | Uo | Zip | Zotz | Tzec | Xul |
| --- | --- | --- | --- | --- | --- |

| Yaxkin | Mol | Chen | Yax | Zac | Ceh | Mac |
| --- | --- | --- | --- | --- | --- | --- |

| Kankin | Muan | Pax | Kayab | Cumhu | Uayeb |
| --- | --- | --- | --- | --- | --- |

Hieroglyphs for the eighteen months of the Maya calendar and the five-day
*Uayeb. (Drawing by Dolona Roberts)*

to the god of the number 8, and so on. Meanwhile the god of Zip
trudges through eternity bearing *his* burden, until it's time to pass it
on to the god of Zotz, the following month.

If it happened that a cycle was picked up by an evil god, bad times
were in store until the cycle was passed on to a friendlier god.
Whether a period was lucky or unlucky depended on the god on
whose back it was carried.

This strange belief helps to explain the power of the priests, the
only ones who could possibly figure out when good gods would make
good things happen and when evil gods might cause things to go
wrong. Forewarned of what might lie ahead, the priests could plan

Imix Ik Akbal

Kan Chicchan Cimi

Manik Lamat Muluc

Oc Chuen Eb

Ben Ix Men

Cib Caban Eznab

Cauac Ahau

Hieroglyphs for the twenty days of the Maya calendar. (*Drawings by Dolona Roberts*)

things to take advantage of lucky periods and cope with the unlucky times—and seemingly managed to convince everyone else that only they stood between normal life and catastrophe.

When modern scholars struggled to understand the complexities of the calendar, the remarkable skills of Maya astronomers became obvious. Using nothing more complicated than a pair of crossed sticks, or perhaps a couple of buildings lined up to provide observation points, they had plotted with amazing precision the movements of the sun, the moon, and Venus, which was of special religious importance to them. For example, they measured the length of the solar year at 365.2420 days, while our present figure is 365.2422. They computed the average revolution of Venus at 584 days; its actual span, as we know it, is 583.92. They studied lunar eclipses and could predict exactly when they would occur.

Calculations as accurate as these had to be based on a sophisticated system of mathematics, and the Maya had one. It included the concept of zero, which no other civilization except the Babylonians and the Hindus had invented. Not even the ancient Greeks had a symbol for "nothing." The zero, which makes it possible to figure large numbers, was unknown in Europe until the Middle Ages, when it was introduced by Arabs who had learned about it from Hindu merchants. It is symbolized in Maya inscriptions as a shell, a hand, or sometimes by glyphs in the form of human heads.

When added to a number, subtracted from a number, multiplied or divided by a number, zero does not change the value of the number. But used *next to* a number, it changes the value a great deal. In our system a zero written to the right of a 3 multiplies it by ten: 30. Two zeros written to the right of a 3 have the effect of multiplying it by a hundred, or ten times ten: 300.

Ours is called a *decimal* system, from the Latin word for ten, on which it is based. The number "235" means two units of 100, three units of 10, and five units of one. The Maya system, based on twenty, is known today as *vigesimal,* from the Latin word for twenty. We write numbers horizontally: 256,817. The Maya wrote their numbers in vertical columns. The ancient Maya used a dot to indicate 1 and a bar to indicate 5. They combined these symbols for numbers from 1 to 19:

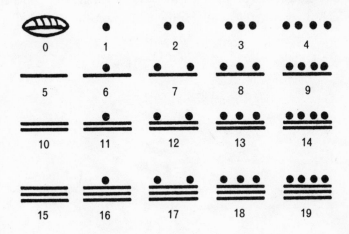

The bar-and-dot numerals used by the Maya.

For numbers of 20 and above, the Maya placed the bar-and-dot and zero figures in vertical columns. Each position going up the column represented a multiplication by 20. The Maya would have written the number 256,817 like this:

$$
\begin{array}{rrr}
1 \text{ unit } & \text{of } 160,000, & \text{or } 160,000 \\
12 \text{ units } & \text{of } 8,000, & \text{or } 96,000 \\
2 \text{ units } & \text{of } 400, & \text{or } 800 \\
0 \text{ units } & \text{of } 20, & \text{or } 0 \\
17 \text{ units } & \text{of } 1, & \text{or } 17 \\
\hline
& & 256,817
\end{array}
$$

The method was amazingly flexible. Although it didn't work for fractions, it could be adapted to multiplication, division, and square roots, but no one knows if the Maya understood these more complicated procedures. Merchants were able to add and subtract speedily, shuffling cacao beans or other counters on the ground like beads on an abacus. Sculptors carved the symbols on monuments to mark the passage of time. And priests used the system to develop the calendar by which they foretold the future and controlled their faithful followers.

PART
THREE


# ANSWERING THE QUESTION:
## WHO
## WERE
## THESE
## PEOPLE?

CHAPTER

VIII

# WHAT
# WAS IT LIKE
# TO BE
# A MAYA?

Knowing that her baby would be born very soon, the expectant mother placed a little stone statue of Ix Chel, the goddess of childbirth, under her bed and called on her for help.

When the baby, a girl, was safely delivered, her parents were joyful. Whether they were rich or poor, the birth of a child was a reason for great rejoicing among the ancient Maya. Children showed how wealthy and fortunate a family really was. The birth of this much-wanted daughter proved that the gods were looking kindly on them.

The day of the tzolkin on which she was born determined which gods were going to favor her, or trouble her, throughout her life. As soon as possible after the birth a priest was called in. He gave her one of her names and cast her horoscope to help her parents in her upbringing. Later she got two more names—a nickname used by her family and close friends and a formal name that was a combination of her parents' family names. Because she was a girl, her name began with *Ix*. Her older brother's name, like all masculine names, began with *Ah*. After a man married, he adopted the prefix *Na*.

Like her parents, the baby girl had coppery brown skin and straight, coarse dark hair. When she grew up, she would probably not be more than four feet eight inches tall (her brother would reach about five feet one inch). At the base of her spine was a small purplish spot that would fade before her tenth birthday. Now called a "Mongolian spot," it is characteristic of Indian groups that trace their prehistoric origins to northeast Asia. The fold of skin at the inner corner of her eyes, known as the "epicanthic eye fold," is another characteristic of the Maya, as it is of several other American Indian groups and of Asiatics.

The Maya thought crossed eyes were beautiful, and so when she was a few weeks old, the little girl's mother attached a ball of resin or a small bead to the hair that hung between the baby's eyes to encourage her eyes to focus inward. The Maya had broad heads and big noses. Shortly after her birth the mother bound the infant's head between two wooden boards, front and back, in order to flatten her forehead and emphasize the long line of her nose, making her more beautiful. When she was older, she would have her earlobes, septum, lips, and one nostril pierced so she could wear a variety of ornaments. Rich and poor alike seemed almost addicted to wearing jewelry. They filed their teeth to sharp points, which they considered elegant, and the wealthy went so far as to inlay their front teeth with bits of jade.

The mother carried her newborn baby in her arms, but when the baby was a few months old the mother shifted her around to sit astride her left hip and supported the child with her left arm. A ceremony still performed among the Maya of Yucatan is the *hetzmek*, when the baby is carried on the mother's hip for the first time. This is done when the girl is three months old (the Maya hearth, symbolic of woman's work in the home, has three stones, and the number three was sacred to women) and for the boy when he is four months old (the cornfield, where the man would work all his life, has four corners).

The parents of the baby girl asked two of their friends to be godparents for her hetzmek. Nine objects, symbolizing what the child would use in adult life, were set out on a mat in the middle of the hut: for a girl, these included such things as a spindle, a bit of cotton, a tiny loom, needles made of bone and cactus thorns, a water jug, a cooking pot, and a *metate*, the stone for grinding maize. The mother handed the baby to her godmother, who set her on her hip and walked around the mat nine times, each time putting one of the objects into the baby's hand and telling her how she would use it. With this ceremony the baby became a member of the community.

Years passed, and when the girl reached the age of five, her mother tied a string around her waist with a red shell dangling from it. A white bead had been braided into her brother's hair when he was the same age. These were symbols of virginity and could not be removed until an elaborate ritual marked the beginning of adolescence.

She was twelve when the rite of passage into adulthood was performed; her brother was fourteen. The priest picked the day, making sure it was not an unlucky one. A leading man of the village was chosen to sponsor the group of children of the same age, to help the priest during the ceremony, and to provide a feast. An old man was appointed the boys' godfather, and an old woman the girls' godmother. Four chacs would assist. Everybody gathered in the court of the sponsor's house, which had been swept clean and spread with fresh leaves. After the priest purified the house and drove out the evil spirits, the house was cleaned again.

The chacs placed a square of white cloth on each child's head, and the priest asked them if they had committed any sins. (A child who confessed to sinning had to leave.) The priest pronounced a benediction, sprinkling water on them with a carved stick with rattlesnake tails attached. Now the sponsor tapped each child on the forehead nine times with a bone given to him by the priest and moistened the forehead and the spaces between the fingers and toes with a mixture of water, ground cacao, and pollen.

The priest removed the cloths from their heads. Then he clipped the beads from the boys' hair, and the mothers cut off the red shells that their daughters had worn. After the children had been dismissed, their parents distributed gifts. The ceremony, called "the descent of the gods," ended with the usual feasting and drinking balche. Bishop Landa would not have approved.

The symbol of purity had been removed and the girl was now of marriageable age. Until she married she lived with her parents and was taught by her mother how to cook, spin cotton yarn, weave, and keep house. She was also learning how a Maya woman should behave. When she passed a man she lowered her eyes, turned her back, and stepped aside. Like her mother, she would never have a meal with her husband; they would not laugh or have long conversations together, and only on rare occasions during certain festivals would they dance with each other.

Meanwhile her brother, like other unmarried men, painted himself black to signify his bachelorhood. He moved out of his parents' home and went to live in a communal house with other young men, where they learned crafts, studied the arts of warfare, and played games. He still spent a great deal of time with his father, with whom he had been going to work in the cornfield since he was very young. There was a sexual double standard: it was assumed that he would keep company with prostitutes, but his sister was expected to be a virgin when she married. Girls who were not chaste were whipped, rubbed with pepper, and publicly ridiculed.

\* \* \*

Ceramic figurine from Jaina, Campeche, showing the typical clothing of a Maya woman of high status. She wears a dress with a cape, a turbanlike headdress, and a large necklace with a pendant. (*Photo by Stuart Rome; courtesy of the National Museum of Anthropology, Mexico*)

There was excitement in the girl's family. A matchmaker had been sent by the father of a young man in the village who wanted her for his wife. In Maya society parents arranged the marriage, sometimes years in advance. The boy's father searched for a wife for his son with the help of a professional matchmaker. Love, the way we think of it, was not a consideration. Marriage was a practical matter. When the time came for having a home and children, a girl was sought who had been properly trained in housekeeping skills and good manners, and proper arrangements were made. The girl was probably fourteen or fifteen when she married; her husband was about eighteen.

There were strict rules about whom one could or could not marry. Men and women were forbidden to marry anyone with the same family name, and there was a list of women a man was not allowed to marry: his mother's sister, his brother's widow, his stepmother, or, if he were a widower, his dead wife's sister.

The matchmaker was offered a drink of cocoa and chili pepper, an expensive beverage usually drunk only by the nobility. After some pleasant socializing, the serious haggling began to settle the matter of the "bride price"—cotton, tobacco, pom, cacao, and so forth—to be given to the girl's family. They also had to agree on the length of time, usually from three to six years, that the young man would have to work for his father-in-law before he could establish his own home. Negotiations were a tricky business, because so much was at stake economically.

Once the details of the marriage had been worked out and the bride's wedding outfit was ready, her parents invited friends and relatives to help build a hut for the couple and to furnish the household things they'd need: pottery for cooking and eating, gourds for water bottles, baskets, wooden chests, woven bags, a metate for grinding maize, and all kinds of tools. This community effort took only two days, with time out for eating and drinking.

When everything was prepared, the ceremony began. The priest led the couple into their new home, lit some copal incense, and built a fire in the hearth. After a short sermon to the young man and woman who sat facing each other on a mat, he left them alone. They sat in silence, looking into the fire until it went out. Meanwhile the festivities continued at the home of the bride's parents.

The next morning before sunrise the new wife got up, lit the fire, and cooked breakfast. She awoke her new husband and shared the breakfast with him. Then he went off to hunt or to work in his father-in-law's fields, and she settled down to her daily routine of grinding corn for their tortillas. That was the beginning of their life together, and it would not change much. The next important event in her life would be the birth of a child. Like her mother, she would place the statue of Ix Chel beneath her bed.

If the marriage was not satisfactory, either the husband or the wife could dissolve it at any time just by declaring that it was ended. Divorce was quite common, and childlessness was one of the main reasons for it. People who had been divorced or widowed did not have a formal wedding ceremony but simply began to live with a new mate and invited their friends and relatives to a banquet to celebrate the new marriage.

Wealthy members of the nobility sometimes had several wives, but peasants were usually monogamous. Maya women had a reputation for jealousy. Landa wrote, "Some carried it so far . . . that they laid hands on the women of whom they are jealous. And so angry and irritated are they . . . that some tear their husband's hair no matter how few times [he] may have been unfaithful." Adultery was a serious offense, and the angry husband had the right to kill his wife's lover by dropping a rock on his head "from a great height." But Landa complained that even with such dire consequences Maya husbands and wives strayed far too often.

\* \* \*

A court scene with a Maya lord seated on a throne and attended by retainers. (*Drawing by Dolona Roberts*)

Of course, almost inevitably, the day came when the wife fell ill. The Maya believed that sickness or any kind of misfortune was the work of evil spirits or a sign of disfavor of the gods. They had a long list of superstitions and saw signs in their dreams. The woman's family called in a sorcerer or priest to examine her, and he prescribed a variety of treatments involving fetishes, rituals, and potions. The potions, made of medicinal herbs, plants, and mineral substances, often cured her. (Sometimes these concoctions included such unappetizing ingredients as bat wings, red worms, animal excrement, urine, blood, crocodile testicles, and bird fat.)

But a time came when none of the remedies worked, and death seemed near. A priest was summoned to hear the woman's final confession and to predict how long she could be expected to live and what prospects loomed ahead for her in the afterlife.

Death terrified the Maya, even though they believed that good people who had obeyed the religious laws were favored by the gods and would eventually go to an eternal paradise somewhere among the thirteen heavens. They thought suicide, especially by hanging, was a great personal sacrifice that guaranteed a place in paradise, along with priests, women who died in childbirth, warriors killed in battle, and victims of sacrifice. People who had done wrong, on the other hand, could expect an eternity of unbearable cold, hunger, and torment by merciless demons in the lowest level of the Underworld.

When the woman died her family buried her in a simple grave under the floor of her hut. Like the noble at Palenque, her body was wrapped in a cotton shroud, sprinkled with cinnabar, and buried either stretched out flat or with the knees drawn up to the chest. Ornaments, pottery containers with offerings of food, and things she had used during her life were put in her grave. Cornmeal and a jade bead placed in her mouth were to provide food and money for the journey to the afterlife. All of these preparations were the same for a man as for a woman. (In northern Yucatan the nobility often cremated their dead, maybe because it was too difficult to dig through the hard limestone surface to prepare underground tombs.) Now the family would abandon the hut and begin their grieving.

Bishop Landa observed their mourning: ". . . it was indeed a thing to see the sorrow and the cries which they made for their dead, and the great grief it caused them. During the day they wept for them in silence; and at night with loud and very sad cries, so that it was pitiful to hear them. And they passed many days in deep sorrow."

# WHAT DID
# THE PEASANTS
# DO ALL DAY?

The Maya farmer takes a step, pokes a hole in the ground with a sharpened stick, drops in a few kernels of corn, kicks dirt over it, takes a step, pokes a hole in the ground. . . .

For perhaps four thousand years, the Maya farmer has planted his *milpa*—cornfield—in exactly this way. The only thing that has changed through all these centuries is the stick; it now has a metal tip.

Corn, more correctly called maize, is and always has been the Maya's most important crop and their main food. Maize is for the Indian peasant what rice is for the Asian and wheat for the European. (Europeans use the word "corn" to refer to a variety of cultivated seed-bearing plants, such as wheat, oats, rye, and barley; "Indian corn" is another term for maize.) Landa wrote, "Truly they almost make a god of it," and he was right. They built their civilization on maize.

And according to a legend in the *Popul Vuh* of Guatemala, maize was their flesh and blood. The charming story of the creation of the world begins by telling how the gods caused the earth to rise out of the seas, how they sculptured the earth's surface into mountains and plains and covered it with plants and living creatures. When the gods saw that the animals and birds had no voices with which to praise them, they created human beings. At first they molded people out of mud, but the rains melted them. Then they carved them out of wood, but the wooden people were drowned by floods; those that survived became monkeys. Finally the gods decided to fashion human beings out of corn, using cobs for arms, legs, and bodies and cornmeal for their flesh. According to the legend, these corn people were the ancestors of the Maya.

That Maya farmer with his pointed stick and sack of maize kernels began, as his forefathers did, by clearing a plot of land. The ancient Maya hacked down the vines and saplings with his stone tools (his descendant uses a steel machete). When the brush was dry—and the priests had decreed that the day was a lucky one—the farmer set fire to the field, a technique known as "slash-and-burn" agriculture. Also called "milpa" or "swidden" agriculture, it is still practiced today.

Just before the summer rains began, probably early in May, he planted the seeds. From May to September he weeded his milpa several times. When the maize was ripe, he bent the stalks down just below the ears to keep the rain from running into the ears and causing mold. Late in the fall, after the kernels had hardened, the farmer began to harvest his crop, taking in what was needed. Depending on where he lived, he either stored the maize on the ear or he shelled the ears in the field and hauled the kernels to the village and stored them in sacks or baskets.

A farmer could grow enough food in four or five months to supply his family and have plenty left over. Today the Maya farmer works only about one hundred and ninety days of the year and raises more

A typical Maya house in Yucatan. Dwellings of this type—with plastered earthen walls and a thatched roof—remained virtually unchanged through Maya history and are still used today.

than twice as much maize as he and his family actually consume; he also feeds some livestock (which he did not have before the Spanish introduced domestic animals) and sells the rest to buy whatever his family can't produce. In prehistoric times, the peasant's surplus maize went to support the nobility and the priesthood, and his surplus time went to build, decorate, and maintain their temples, palaces, roadways, and residences.

Each year the milpa yielded less maize, and after a few seasons, the soil was depleted. The farmer cleared a new field, leaving the old one to lie dormant. This technique required a lot of land, because so much of it was unusable. Only about a fifth of the land was being farmed at any given time. Scholars wondered how a civilization as complex as the Maya could have been supported by such an inefficient system. Now they know that although milpas were important for growing certain staple crops, other techniques were employed too, especially during the Classic period when the population was increasing.

In some lowland areas they turned swamps and river floodplains into raised fields by piling up the soil between ditches to create extremely fertile plots. In hilly places they built stone-walled terraces to keep the soil from being washed away. They probably learned to rotate their crops, to grow several kinds of produce at the same time in the same field, and to raise a succession of crops during one growing season. They also planted orchards and small gardens near their houses, as they do today.

Maize was first with the Maya; beans were second—red and black varieties often planted in the same holes with the corn and allowed to grow up around the cornstalks. Beans provided protein and were cooked with chili peppers, a source of vitamin C. Farmers raised squash and pumpkin, sweet potatoes, tomatoes, cassava (also called manioc, a starchy root that yields flour; tapioca is made from it), avocadoes, *chayote* (a fruit similar to summer squash), *jicama* (a root resembling a turnip, eaten raw), *chaya* (the leaves were boiled), and other vegetables. They picked bananas, plantains (similar to bananas), papaya (a fruit like a melon eaten raw or cooked), and several kinds of nuts, all growing wild.

The ancient Maya planted breadnut trees around their villages, as their descendants do. The outer covering of the breadnut is sweet, and the seeds are boiled and eaten as a vegetable—another source of protein—or dried and ground into flour. Today the leaves of the tree are used for fodder for mules and horses.

They harvested cacao (the source of cocoa and chocolate), tobacco, gourds, rubber (natural latex extracted from the *Castilla* tree), vanilla, and pom, the resin of the copal tree. They raised cotton extensively, since most of their clothing was made of cotton. Henequen (also called hemp or sisal) was used to make rope, for many years the only export of the Yucatan Peninsula. There are still henequen plantations throughout Yucatan, but the business has dwindled because of the demand for synthetic fiber.

The Maya were primarily vegetarians. Edward Thompson studied the ancient kitchen middens (refuse heaps) at Chichen Itza as well as what the modern Maya ate. He found that through the ages the Maya based about eighty percent of their diet on maize. Vegetables represented another twelve percent, and meat, which was usually reserved for special occasions, accounted for eight percent. In ancient times the only domesticated animals besides dogs, which they sometimes ate, were turkeys and ducks; other meat depended on hunter's luck. Coastal dwellers had plentiful seafood. Stingless bees, common to the area, kept in hives inside hollow logs, provided honey. (Coffee, cane sugar, and animals like cows, pigs, and chickens came with the Spanish.) And of course a portion of all of this bounty belonged to the nobility, on whose land the peasant lived and worked.

The bread of the Maya has always been and still is made of ground maize formed into thin cakes called *tortillas*, the Spanish name for pancakes. Cooking, and especially making tortillas, was and is the peasant wife's main activity. First she soaked the hard, dry kernels of maize overnight in limewater to soften the hulls. The next morning she washed off the hulls and ground the grains into a thick dough called *zacan* on a smooth stone metate. When it was close to time for

Maya farmers tending a field of maize. The figure on the right is carrying a digging stick. (*Drawing by Dolona Roberts*)

Scenes from murals discovered in a temple at Bonampak, Chiapas:
(a) a group of five *batabs* or lords in ceremonial attire;
(b) musicians playing turtleshell carapaces, a drum, and rattles.

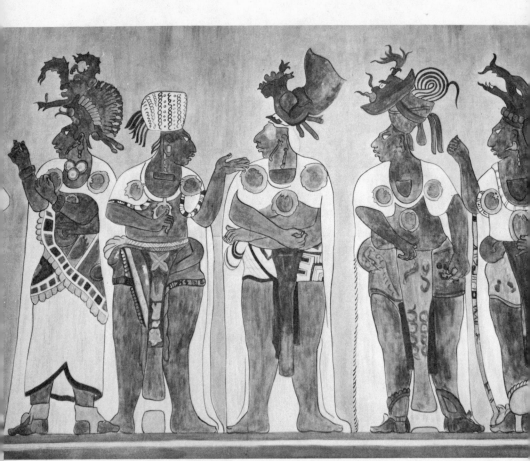

the main meal, she took a lump of zacan and patted it into a round,
thin, flat cake and baked it on a round stone griddle placed on the
stone hearth.

Today the Maya housewife takes her corn to the village mill for grinding and carries away the dough in a bucket. If she is really a modern woman, she may have a press to make the family's tortillas, unless her husband insists that she pat them by hand, the way it was always done. The average Maya man eats nearly twenty tortillas at one meal.

Copan

Seibal

Naranjo

Piedras Negras

Quirigua

Palenque

Tikal

Yaxchilan

Emblem glyphs of Maya cities. (*Redrawn from Berlin by Dolona Roberts*)

The Maya farmer, meanwhile, who has been laboring in his milpa since daybreak, pauses occasionally for a snack. He mixes a lump of zacan with water to make a drink called *pozole*. (A thicker mixture of zacan and water, served hot and sometimes sweetened with honey, is known as *atole*.) When he comes back from the fields, he expects his meal to be ready and his tortillas hot.

One difference between ancient and modern Maya eating habits seems to be the time of the main meal. Formerly it was "an hour before sunset"; now it is usually noon or early afternoon. Whenever it is, the women today serve stews, tamales (corn mush with a spicy filling wrapped in dried cornhusks and steamed), chili, beans, vegetables, fruit, and maybe some chocolate, if they can afford it—and, of course, stacks and stacks of tortillas kept hot in a gourd. The men and women eat separately, as they always have—the men first, seated on mats or low wooden stools. After the men have been fed, the women and girls eat their meal, saving the leftover tortillas to be toasted for breakfast the next day.

The Maya farmer working in his milpa today dresses in trousers and a shirt, sandals, and a straw hat over his short haircut. His ancestors, however, wore nothing but a loincloth called an *ex,* a narrow strip of woven cotton long enough to wind around his waist and pass between his legs. He had a square cloth to wrap around his shoulders; this *pati* also served as a blanket for sleeping. He pulled his long hair back and burned a bare spot at the top of his head, and he went to great pains to decorate his body with tattoos and decorative scars.

The modern Maya wife wears a square-cut dress with embroidery around the neck and the hem, called a *huipile.* This dress is much like the dresses her ancestors wore. Like them, she drapes a *rebozo* around her neck and shoulders. But she no longer decorates her body with tattoos and scars and body paint as she would have centuries ago. Women of that time braided their luxuriant hair in a variety of styles and sometimes decorated it with ornaments.

The day begins early, and it ends early too. Everyone goes to sleep in a hut almost identical to the huts in which their ancestors lived. Oval, square, or rectangular, it is made of poles tied together with vines and plastered with mud; nails have never been used. The steeply pitched roof is thatched with palm leaves. The floor is of packed earth. Basically a single room, the interior is divided by high partitions into two sections, one part for sleeping. Cool, airy hammocks are a modern invention; Maya ancestors slept on beds made of saplings and covered with mats. The tropical night passes, and when the sun again ascends the sky, the Maya family will rise with it and go about their daily chores as they have for thousands of years.

# WHAT ABOUT
# THE
# UPPER CLASSES?

ilently, secretly, like shy animals, the Lacandon Indians melted into the jungle. After the Spaniards came in the sixteenth century, this Maya tribe had chosen to disappear rather than to resist. An effort to Christianize them in 1790 failed completely; after that they were forgotten by the outside world. Isolated in the impenetrable jungle, the Lacandon hid themselves from the slow poison of outside influence.

But by the middle of the twentieth century, *chicleros* (gatherers of chicle, the juice used to make chewing gum), mahogany cutters, and oil prospectors had infiltrated parts of the state of Chiapas. Many young Indian men had gone to bigger towns to look for work. The Lacandon began to decline. Only a few hundred were left, clinging stubbornly to the primitive lifestyle of their ancestors, which had survived through centuries of isolation. Without really understanding

Aerial view of Tikal, Guatemala, showing the Central Plaza with Temple I
(top), Temple II (bottom right), and the North Acropolis. (*Courtesy of the
University Museum, University of Pennsylvania*)

why they were doing it, except that they always had, they carried out rituals and made offerings of maize, balche, and pom in deserted temples amid the ruins of Maya cities.

Then in 1946 an author-explorer named Giles G. Healey accepted an assignment from the United Fruit Company to make a documentary film about the Maya. Healey traced the Lacandon to their remote villages. He noticed that the men of one village retreated regularly to a shrine somewhere in the rain forest. He asked to go with them, but the secretive Lacandon were reluctant to let him. Finally he persuaded them, in exchange for shotguns and ammunition, to take him to the shrine. They led him along narrow trails through jungle so thick in places that no direct sunlight reached the earth, and without his guides Healey might have passed by the ruins without ever knowing they were there.

Eventually they reached the crumbled remains of temples, palaces, platforms, monuments, and intricately carved stelae, all engulfed by the jungle. On a high terrace stood a plain, flat-roofed building which, even with a heavy drapery of trees and vines, was still in remarkably good shape. Three doorways opened into three small rooms.

Ducking through one of the doorways, Healey entered a narrow room with a vaulted ceiling. As he grew accustomed to the dim light, he became aware of a multitude of faces and figures on the walls, an incredible collection of gorgeously costumed priests, nobles, warriors, musicians, and masked characters. Healey discovered an incredible display of murals covering the walls of all three rooms, the most extensive paintings—and the most realistic—yet found anywhere in Mesoamerica.

Most Maya wall paintings (those at Chichen Itza are a notable exception) deal with symbols; these deal with life. Painted between A.D. 760 and 800, they illustrate Maya life near the end of the Classic period, when the civilization was at its peak. At the suggestion of

Temple II at Tikal as it appeared about A.D. 700. Note the roof comb embellished with sculpture. (*Reconstruction drawing by Tatiana Proskouriakoff; courtesy of the University of Oklahoma Press*)

Sylvanus Morley, the site was named Bonampak, meaning "painted walls."

A religious ceremony is in progress in the murals in the first room. A group of nobles in full ceremonial regalia includes the supreme ruler surrounded by his family. Nearby, a troupe of dancers are dressing in costumes decorated with bright quetzal feathers. On the lower panel a group of masked actors is accompanied by a band of musicians playing their instruments: trumpets, rattles, a drum, and tortoise shells on which they're beating with deer antlers.

The second room continues with a raid to capture human victims and their ceremonial sacrifice on the stairs of a temple building. One scene shows the attack by elaborately clothed warriors. In the next scene the captives, stripped to their loincloths, kneel or sit before the haughty chieftains, waiting to hear what their fate may be.

The third room portrays the climax, a dance in magnificent costumes on the steps of a pyramid, and a bloodletting ceremony by the high priest and his family. In the midst of them the body of a captive is held by the hands and feet while a priest flails the corpse. A group of chiefs dressed in long white capes appear to be watching from the opposite wall and discussing the sacrifice. Below them minor officials sit cross-legged, talking animatedly.

The paintings show the fabulous costumes made from intricately woven fabrics, feathers, cut stone, and furs. Headdresses of delicate featherwork are nearly as tall as the people who wear them. Loincloths are richly embroidered around the waist, and feathers dangle from the ends in front and back. Sandals, whether of leather or woven fiber, are incredibly ornate. And the figures are decked out in all kinds of jewelry: rings, breastplates, pendants, necklaces, earplugs, and nose-ornaments made of jade, jaguar claws, shell, alligator teeth, and bone.

Over the centuries, before Healy came, water had seeped through the limestone walls, leaving a heavy coating that preserved the paintings but also obscured many of the details—a problem until it was found that a treatment of kerosene made the deposit translucent. Originally the murals had been painted on an undercoating of lime plaster. The figures were first drawn on the plaster in red and the outlines filled in with colors made from various vegetables and minerals. The artists used brushes made of animal hair or feathers.

The scenes tell a story, and the style is so realistic that the faces of certain characters can be recognized from room to room as they reappear in different parts of the story. The mood changes from one scene to the next: the characters seem relaxed as they get ready for the raid, look ferocious in the fighting, appear cold and forbidding as they sacrifice their victim.

The Bonampak murals show the Maya priests and nobles busy in their public lives. They also provide some new information. The presence of the wife and children of the chief priest challenges the old idea that only men attended these ceremonies. And the belief that human sacrifice was rare before postclassic times is questioned, since it obviously happened regularly at Bonampak.

"A sort of pictorial encyclopedia of a Maya city of the eighth century," is the way French anthropologist Jacques Soustelle described Bonampak. "The city comes to life there again, with its ceremonies and its processions, its stiff and solemn-looking dignitaries weighed down by their heavy plumed adornments, its warriors clothed in jaguar skins. Lively or violent scenes are there displayed side by side with gracious, familiar pictures of daily life. A complete cross-section of society—women, children, servants, musicians, warrior chiefs, dying prisoners, and masked dancers—that is what these painters . . . succeeded in depicting on those walls, lost today in the depths of one of the continent's most impenetrable jungles. . . ."

Hieroglyphics date the murals near the end of the eighth century. Shortly after that date, Bonampak was abandoned, leaving the motionless figures to stare down at empty rooms until Giles Healey discovered them twelve centuries later.

Once again, the ubiquitous Bishop Landa is the source of much that we know about Maya nobility, called the *almehenob*, such as that pictured at Bonampak. Like the priests, they were divided into several classes, each with special duties. The highest ranking noble was the *halac uinic* or "true man." Each major city was governed by one of these nobles, who also had some ceremonial duties. He may have been a priest who was looked up to as a kind of god-king, and he was regarded with such awe that a cloth was always held in front of his face so that no one could talk directly to him. When he died his oldest son or brother inherited his position, but if he had no heir a successor was chosen from one of the noble families.

Next came minor chieftains called *batabs* (meaning "axe bearers"), picked by the halac uinic from among noble families. They were somewhat like town mayors, whose job was to oversee local government and collect tributes from the peasants. There were no prisons, but batabs acted as judges and handed out sentences. Murder was punished by death unless it was accidental; then the defendant was fined a certain amount of cotton cloth or cacao beans. A thief was made the slave of his victim, and less important crimes were punished with short haircuts as a sign of disgrace.

Below the batabs were administrative assistants and councillors and constables who enforced laws. There were also men who presided over public meetings and conducted rehearsals for certain kinds of festivals, dances, and chants. All of them either inherited their posts or were chosen on the basis of family status. Many of the almehenob were merchants who owned land and slaves and controlled trade and natural resources.

Now that scholars have learned to read more hieroglyphics, they have been able to reconstruct the names, dates, and relationships of ruling families of several important centers. They know, for instance, that the noble whose tomb Alberto Ruz discovered at Palenque was a man named Pacal, which means "shield," and that he ruled Palenque from A.D. 615 to 683. His wife, Ahpo Hel, may have also been his sister; his son, Chan Bahlum, inherited Pacal's control over the city the year after his father's death. A man named Bird Jaguar once governed Yaxchilan in Guatemala, and others with picturesque names like Curl Snout and Stormy Sky were powerful rulers at Tikal. Lists of kings and even a few queens have been compiled for a number of major cities, with information on when they were born, came to power, and died, and on the political alliances they formed with the rulers of nearby cities.

The almehenob lived their lives at one end of the social scale, but they didn't treat harshly the people at the other end, the *yalba uinicob* —"lesser men." And some peasants, at least, may have been able to move up on the scale to become minor bureaucrats, merchants, craftsmen, and technicians. As the big centers got even bigger, they probably included a large population of such people.

Nobody knows much about systems of government during the Classic period. A few major centers had some control over smaller neighboring cities. "Emblem glyphs" are hieroglyphic symbols standing for either the names of individual cities or their ruling dynasties. Often the emblem glyph of a major city like Tikal or Copan shows up in the art of smaller neighboring centers. This probably indicated that these cities had some kind of tie—royal marriages, military alliances for protection, or economics, for instance—and were not completely independent with their own halac uinicob. But this network of cities was probably never formed into one empire with a supreme ruler.

Warriors in the Bonampak paintings parade in their gorgeous headdresses, jewelry, and jaguar-skin capes, and their attendants blow wooden trumpets and hold colorful banners and parasols over their heads. War was a kind of ritual, always accompanied by ceremonies to appeal to the gods for help. Raids and minor skirmishes went on all the time. Before every campaign the women cooked and packed food for the troops to carry on their backs. The men painted their faces red, black, and white, and marched into battle to the beat of drums and the blast of conch shell trumpets. They carried shields made of stiff deer or jaguar hide and short spears with flint or obsidian points, wooden clubs, and flint knives. They also had slings for hurling rocks and "hornet bombs"—nests of hornets that broke open when they landed among the enemy troops. (They did not have the bow and arrow until near the end of their history, when these weapons were introduced by intruders from Mexico.)

The fighting did not begin until an image of the war god was brought out and both armies had gone through their rituals and paid their respects to each other. They never fought at night—a truce was declared at sundown until the next morning. But once the battle had begun they fought fiercely. To prove their skill, victorious warriors displayed on their arms the jawbones of the enemy dead. Killing or capturing an enemy officer was a heroic deed. But the main goal was to take prisoners, high-ranking officers and nobles to be used for sacrifice and common soldiers for slavery.

Yet warfare did not seem to disrupt daily life. During the six centuries of the Classic period the population of the lowlands grew, cities were expanded, and trade went on without interruption.

Ancient Maya markets were probably as crowded and noisy as those of the present, while merchants did a brisk business in local products as well as items imported from other areas on the backs of slaves. Feathers and animal skins, honey and beeswax, pom and rubber, local pottery, and other products of the lowlands were exchanged for such highland specialties as jade, obsidian, cinnabar, and *their* style of pottery. Traders from the seacoast offered salt, dried fish, shells, stingray spines, and pearls to inlanders. Cacao beans were used for money, but stone or shell beads, red beans, or feathers were also forms of currency. Markets were, as well, meeting places where people gathered and exchanged ideas with visitors from other areas. There may have been games of chance when people got together to trade and talk. One popular marketplace game was played by throwing "dice"—kernels of dried corn painted with black marks—and betting on how they would fall.

Thriving commerce was a vital and vibrant part of Maya civilization. Landa observed that "the occupation to which they had the greatest inclination was trade." But then, like the rest of Maya life, it all came to an end.

PART
FOUR

# THE ULTIMATE QUESTION:
# WHAT
# HAPPENED

CHAPTER

XI


# THE
# PUZZLE
# OF THE
# DESERTED CITIES


And now comes the biggest mystery of all: the collapse of Maya civilization. No one knows exactly what happened, or why.

Over the course of a century, from about A.D. 800 to 900, the Maya disappeared from their bustling cities throughout the southern lowland area, apparently simply vanishing into the jungle. They left behind unfinished buildings and monuments, and in one city after another they stopped erecting stelae. The sequence of dates carved on these monuments has made it possible to follow the path of the decline in artistic, intellectual, and religious activity. Once the Maya had gone, it did not take long for the rain forest to reclaim those magnificent cities, for vines and trees to surround the temples and palaces, and for roots to split stones and crush walls.

A number of theories have been suggested. Perhaps invading

armies from Mexico killed many of the Maya and the rest had fled from the conquerors. The Mexicans were extremely warlike, but there was no real evidence that this had happened. Other rejected notions had to do with changes in climate, earthquakes, disease epidemics, and an imbalance in the ratio of women to men that might have caused a drop in the birthrate.

Sylvanus Morley's theory was "agricultural exhaustion." He believed that the milpa system, continually clearing new lands while others lay unused, was wasteful and couldn't produce enough food to keep up with the growing population. But later researchers found that the Maya were much more efficient farmers than Morley thought. And it seems that lowland cities were abandoned hastily; "agricultural exhaustion" was a slow process.

Almost completely hidden by the jungle of Guatemala lies the city of Piedras Negras, its monuments among the finest ever carved by Maya sculptors. One outstanding piece is a raised platform or dais that was once used as a throne. At some time—no one is sure when—this dais was intentionally smashed. A sculptured wall panel showing a high priest or ruler presiding over a group of almehenob had been deliberately destroyed, the head of each figure broken off. Vandalized stelae and altars have been dug up at Tikal; one called the "Red Stela," because it had been painted red, was shattered and the pieces buried under the temple floor.

Mayanists guessed that this destruction was evidence of a peasant uprising. Perhaps the hard-working people simply got tired of the endless demands of priests and rulers for more buildings, more ceremonies, more tributes, more luxuries, more of everything. Something—a crop failure, a disaster that the priests failed to deal with—might then have urged the weary peasants to rebel and abandon the cities.

Today, experts believe there was no single cause for the decline, but a complex combination of reasons. By the end of the Classic period the powerful priests and wealthy nobles controlled the economy, especially foreign trade. They probably determined how food and raw materials were to be distributed. It was up to the peasants to feed and support the elite, which seemed to be growing larger and more complicated all the time.

Meanwhile, the general population was also increasing and the cities getting larger. It is estimated, for instance, that Tikal had between twenty-five thousand and fifty thousand inhabitants at that time. Competition between major centers intensified as they tried to outdo each other in putting up magnificent buildings and dressing in elaborate clothing and jewelry. Eventually the rivalry may even have erupted in fighting among the cities, and wars required manpower and food to support them.

This combination put a huge burden on all their resources, all the more draining since the Maya probably didn't have the technology to deal with these demands. (They still of course did not have wheels, draft animals, or metal tools.) These problems created what some scholars have called "stress factors" that left the Maya civilization dangerously weak. At that point all it would have taken was some situation like famine or disease to set off a disastrous chain reaction. And if all of these "stress factors" happened to come together at one time, the result was chaos.

Another theory lays the blame on outside influences. Pottery found at sites in the Guatemalan lowlands indicates that outsiders came to the area in the ninth century, either directly from Mexico or from Yucatan, where the Maya had already been affected by Mexican culture. But nobody knows if this was a military invasion or a gradual immigration of people with different ideas. Whatever it was, it was the last straw. The Maya crumbled under a combination of outside pressures and internal tensions. Whatever happened, never again would Maya civilization shine in its former brilliance.

The next question is, what happened to the survivors? Excavations at Uaxactun and Tikal showed that people continued to live in and around those cities long after they stopped functioning as major centers. They even lived in some of the buildings and used them as burial places. Looters broke into many of Tikal's rich tombs, and a few of its stelae and altars were hauled off and set up in other locations.

The population in the southern lowlands declined steadily from the end of the tenth century. A few small, semi-isolated groups stayed behind and made half-hearted attempts to use the deserted temples, probably to keep in touch with their ancient gods. Without an educated elite or strong priesthood to guide them, the art and architecture they produced were only a poor imitation of what they had once accomplished. At Tikal the links with the past were so weak that Indians who remained sometimes put monuments in place upside down or backwards, as if they had forgotten how to read their hieroglyphic inscriptions.

But this was not true in northern Yucatan, where Maya civilization survived long after it had collapsed in the south. For a long time experts believed that refugees from southern cities migrated to the upper half of the peninsula, which they thought had been largely uninhabited during the Classic period. Then between A.D. 900 and 1200 these newcomers had built magnificent new cities in a kind of resurgence of Maya tradition. Chichen Itza is the best known; others such as Uxmal, Kabah, Sayil, Labna, and many more make up one of the most spectacular arrays of ancient ruins anywhere in the New World. But the discovery of dated inscriptions and pottery in the area showed that even before the southern lowlands were deserted, Yucatan was inhabited by people who knew about hieroglyphics and calendar-making. The idea of a new burst of energy fueled by immigrants was abandoned. This was the work of established groups.

Architecture in the upper Yucatan Peninsula differed dramatically from that of the lowlands. Buildings were less formally arranged, and there were fewer terraced pyramids. Stone columns supported doorways, and ornate decorations on the faces of buildings replaced the lowland's elegant, comparatively simple style. This was not a new trend in architecture; some of it was a natural regional variation that had begun to develop much earlier.

Most of these cities were thriving in Yucatan at the same time as those farther to the south. Nearly all of their art and architecture had their roots in Classic traditions. And it may even be that when the southern cities were abandoned, many of Yucatan's centers were also deserted. Not everyone agrees; one group of scholars believes that northern Yucatan cities didn't really begin to flourish until late in the Classic period and continued to thrive for several centuries afterward, somehow surviving the downfall to the south.

No matter which is true, a completely different force now swept over the Maya. In the midst of all the changes that were going on, the civilization got a new stimulus from some outside source. It shows up in much of the architecture at Chichen Itza with its distinctly non-Maya flavor. The famous ruins of Chichen Itza represent Maya civilization in the minds of thousands of tourists who visit them every year, but actually some of its architecture is completely out of keeping with traditional Maya thinking.

Nothing like the square platforms at Chichen Itza and in nearby ruins had ever been seen in the Maya area, but they're similar to platforms found in central Mexico. Murals on the walls and columns at Chichen Itza show warriors wearing quilted cotton armor and carrying shields, spears and spear-throwers, and clubs tipped with flint or obsidian, not at all like the usual images portrayed by Maya artists. Huge columns carved in the form of feathered serpents, rows

Chichen Itza as it may have appeared about A.D. 1100. In the center stands the Temple of Kukulcan in front of which a causeway leads to the Well of Sacrifice; to the left is the Temple of the Warriors; on the right is the Ball Court. (*Reconstruction drawing by Tatiana Proskouriakoff; courtesy of the University of Oklahoma Press*)

of eagles and crouching jaguars with human hearts in their claws, and figures called *chac mools*, men lying on their backs with knees and head raised—all these are characteristics associated with the Toltec culture that once dominated central Mexico. These foreign

The Temple of Kukulcan, Chichen Itza. Although it is one of the best known Maya buildings, it shows strong Toltec influences from central Mexico. Note, for example, the heads of feathered serpents at the bottom of the stairway, images of the powerful Mexican deity Quetzalcoatl, whom the Maya called Kukulcan.

traits were probably marks left by Toltec invaders who conquered the city.

Myths abounded in Mexican folklore concerning the Toltecs, their legendary capital, Tollan, and their priest-king, the famous Quetzalcoatl. But for years nobody could say for sure who the Toltecs were or if Tollan had ever actually existed. Then, in the 1940s, archaeologists digging near the small town of Tula, some fifty-four miles northwest of Mexico City, discovered that most of the characteristics identified with Chichen Itza existed here too: columns, chac mools, and feathered serpents that were the emblem of Quetzalcoatl. Rows of carved skulls on monuments and walls demonstrated the Toltecs' obsession with human sacrifice. There were so many similarities that it was almost as though the same artists and architects created both Tula and Chichen Itza. And it was now certain that Tula and Tollan were once the same.

It seems that the Toltecs had come from various places in Mexico over a period of several centuries and settled at Tula. Their power and influence spread. In the tenth century, a large number of people left Tula, under the leadership of Quetzalcoatl. They eventually arrived in Yucatan and settled at Chichen Itza. By some time in the twelfth century, as a result of internal conflicts, Tula was abandoned.

The remarkable deeds of Quetzalcoatl were described in myths. His name combines the Mexican words *quetzal*, the magnificently plumed bird, and *coatl*, meaning snake, and he was always shown as a feathered serpent. In addition to being a culture hero, he was an extremely important god, the patron of art, literature, agriculture, and science, idolized throughout Mexico and Central America for his wisdom and gentleness.

Quetzalcoatl's fame spread far and wide. The Maya of Yucatan called him Kukulcan. Landa reported, "It is believed among the Indians that with the Itzas who occupied Chichen Itza there reigned a great lord named Kukulcan, and that the principal building [the

Temple of Kukulcan] shows this to be true. . . . They say that he was favorably disposed, and had no wife or children . . .; and they also considered him a god in Yucatan on account of his being a just statesman; and this is seen in the order which he imposed on Yucatan after the death of the lords, in order to calm the dissensions which their deaths had caused in the country."

Could such a man actually have existed? Historians believe that Quetzalcoatl was an important deity in Mexico, before the Toltecs arrived on the scene, and that an early Toltec chieftain, possibly a whole series of them, may have taken his name as a way of making themselves seem even more powerful. The worship of Quetzalcoatl-Kukulkan was, without doubt, carried into Yucatan by the tide of Mexican culture that moved through the area during the tenth century, although archaeologists do not agree on when and how.

Once a year every city in Yucatan held a festival to honor Kukulcan. It began with a parade of lavishly dressed priests, nobles, and special clowns. Colorful feather banners fluttered on temple tops. Offerings of food and clay idols were placed in the courtyard below. Fasting, prayers, and dances went on for five days, and the clowns performed in the streets to collect gifts for the priests and lords who took part in the rites.

The origin of a group called the Itza has long puzzled archaeologists. The Itza supposedly settled at Chichen Itza (the name means "well of the Itza") in the tenth century and developed it into a powerful center. Maya chronicles written after the Conquest described the Itza as "foreigners," "tricksters," and "those who speak our language brokenly." But no one knows where they came from or even if they were actually Toltec. Some say the Itza was a tribe of Mayan-speaking people from the coast of Tabasco (north of Chiapas) and Campeche who had already absorbed strong Mexican influences. These people settled at Chichen Itza around A.D. 918, and when Quetzalcoatl and his Toltec followers arrived some seventy years

A view of Chichen Itza showing a structure known as "La Iglesia" in the
foreground, a typical example of the Puuc style of architecture decorated
with cut stone and long-nosed masks of the rain god Chac. In the background
can be seen a building with a round tower which is believed to have been
used as an astronomical observatory.

later, they were warmly welcomed. But another theory claims that the Itza did not arrive from Mexico until the thirteenth century, long after the Toltecs had made themselves at home there.

Whichever way it happened, the new groups took over, sometimes by force. Some cities were abandoned, but others continued to flourish under the new regime. Chichen Itza was well located to be the conquerors' capital, and other cities around it became centers of their authority.

There were other changes. Gold, copper, and turquoise were imported from Mexico, and two distinctive kinds of pottery appeared. Warfare and warriors increased in importance. New gods and ceremonies were introduced, and human sacrifice became far more common than it had ever been. The Maya willingly accepted this different religion. In time, the Toltecs influenced almost every aspect of Maya culture; new artistic styles, religious beliefs, and customs blended with older traditions. Maya technology and craftsmanship continued to surface in all the Toltec-inspired work, and remnants of Maya civilization survived even after the great Classic tradition had ended.

Chichen Itza was the focus of artistic, religious, and economic activity in Yucatan for over two hundred years, but the chain of events stretching from about A.D. 1200 until the Spanish Conquest is hazy. After Chichen Itza lost status, the Itza under the leadership of Kukulcan founded a new capital at Mayapan, thirty miles southeast of Merida. The land was divided among the lords who lived within its walls.

During a sacrifice at the Sacred Well at Chichen Itza, Hunac Ceel, a powerful lord of Mayapan, was among the people thrown into the pool. No one knows why he was being sacrificed—maybe he volunteered, or he might have jumped in after the other victims failed to bring back any message from the underwater gods. Whichever way it happened, Hunac Ceel swam to the surface and shouted to the onlookers that he had conversed with the gods and they had given him their prophecy. This dramatic act so impressed the crowd that they hauled him out of the cenote and made him their ruler.

Next Hunac Ceel decided to get rid of his chief rival, Chac Xib Chac, the reigning chieftain of Chichen Itza. How he managed this is also unclear, but after it was done, Chichen Itza was overrun and eventually abandoned, and Mayapan became the most powerful city in Yucatan. Hunac Ceel and his descendants controlled most of the northern part of the peninsula for two and a half centuries, until the walled city was overthrown and burned around the middle of the fifteenth century.

In 1951 the Carnegie Institution sponsored a project to excavate Mayapan's main buildings, a huge job since the site covered almost two square miles with 4140 structures. The evidence brought to light showed that many people—nobles, craftsmen, and peasants—lived inside its walls. Religion was no longer so important. Small shrines took the place of major religious buildings, and those that did exist were crudely built. In other parts of Yucatan art and architecture declined, and emphasis on warfare and production of cheap merchandise increased.

The area was in turmoil. Yucatan was split up into sixteen independent provinces, each governed by its own chieftain with his own private army. Rulers came and went, sometimes ousted by conspiracies, sometimes by assassination. The story was essentially the same everywhere, and no leaders emerged to halt the decline.

Nobody knows if the chaos into which the Maya had lapsed would have been fatal had the conquistadors not appeared on the scene. Some say the culture was doomed, but others argue that it might have emerged in a new form. We will never know. The arrival of the Spanish marked the final chapter of Maya civilization.

# CHAPTER
## XII

# THE
# SEARCH
# GOES ON

Brilliant achievements, exciting revelations, and countless unsolved mysteries—this is the legacy left by the ancient Maya. Huge areas remain to be explored, dozens of key sites to be investigated. There are hieroglyphic inscriptions to decipher and mountains of data to analyze. And so there are always new projects, new digs, new studies—and new breakthroughs.

In 1962 a geologist prospecting for an oil company in the jungle of Guatemala came across a cluster of ruins. He got in touch with Richard E. W. Adams, a young archaeologist who was on a dig in another part of the country. At that time all the two could do was to map the Rio Azul site, named for a river nearby. There was no money then to excavate the ruins they had found.

Over the next twenty years thieves dug trenches around the pyramids, tunneled into them, and even split them open to get at the treasures inside. The looters ransacked at least twenty-eight tombs in this and the surrounding area, smuggling jewelry and other priceless objects into the United States where they were sold to art collectors for huge sums of money. When Adams returned to Rio Azul in 1981 he heard about the looting and saw the deep trenches and the scattered rubble. On one occasion he and another scientist surprised armed looters at work. Shots were fired and one of the thieves was wounded, but they all got away. After that incident Guatemalan government troops swept the area, and guards with automatic weapons have remained on duty ever since to prevent further looting.

When artifacts are stolen and sold, all the valuable information they could provide is lost forever. Adams and other archaeologists used this incident to convince Congress to pass a law to stop national treasures looted in other countries from being brought into the United States. In addition the U.S. signed an agreement that commits this country to recover and return stolen Guatemalan cultural and archaeological objects.

Meanwhile, Adams raised the money to begin excavating the ruin in a race against the looters. The ancient city of Rio Azul was probably a small center under the control of the bigger city of Tikal, a few miles to the south. It covers about four hundred and seventy acres and contains four major temple pyramids and adjoining smaller buildings. Adams and his team had been working on the site for several weeks in the spring of 1984, hoping to get as much accomplished as possible before the rainy season began. Then on May fifteenth a workman's leg plunged through rock and dirt fill down through the roof of a secret chamber, a cave cut into the rock some thirteen feet below the surface of the ground. Hidden by a wing of a temple built on top of it, the cave had gone undetected by looters— and until then by archaeologists as well.

One of the expedition leaders peered in. "It's painted!" he yelled; whoops of excitement greeted the announcement. They began working furiously to clear the rubble from the entrance to what they knew was a tomb. Next they lowered a miniature video camera into the opening. And finally, using vines and saplings from the jungle—traditional Maya building materials—they climbed down into the chamber.

The skeleton of a nobleman in his thirties, his shroud nothing more than dust, lay on a wooden bier. Elaborate and mysterious wall paintings and fifteen pieces of pottery surrounded his body. One of the pieces is a beautifully made jar with an unusual screw-top lid. On top of the skeleton lay a stingray spine used in bloodletting rituals. Parrots chattered overhead and Guatemalan government guards with

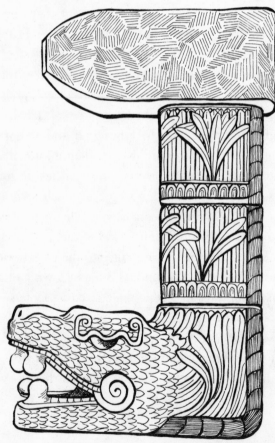

Feathered serpent column representing Quetzalcoatl or Kukulcan, Temple of the Jaguars, Chichen Itza. (*Drawing by Dolona Roberts*)

rifles and machetes stood by as the contents of Tomb 19, as it was now designated, were recorded and labeled and then transported to the National Museum of Anthropology in Guatemala City.

The date of the tomb is about A.D. 420 to 470, the height of the Classic period. Adams, who calls it "a moment frozen in time," believes that the tomb was built for a relative of a ruler buried in a large pyramid nearby, already looted and stripped of its wall paintings. All that could be read of the hieroglyphics on the walls and pottery were the words "Great Son."

Maya tombs that have survived looting and damage by the humidity of the jungle are extremely rare. Tomb 19 at Rio Azul is one of the most notable discoveries since Alberto Ruz painstakingly burrowed his way into the intact tomb in Palenque in 1952. The wall paintings at Rio Azul are better preserved than those at Bonampak, where leaking water had left a mineral deposit.

"It's a time capsule that reflects the behavior patterns of the period," said Richard Adams, one of the world's leading Maya scholars and part of the new breed of archaeologists. Described as "a tall man with a striking mustache and flashing eyes and a commanding presence," he studied anthropology but ended up with a job selling mutual funds. Eventually, though, Mayismo got him. He gave up sales and went to Harvard to work on a graduate degree in archaeology. He has spent years of hard labor in the field, earning a name for himself by his innovative research methods and new ways of interpreting the evidence.

In the late 1970s the National Aeronautics and Space Administration was testing its new imaging radar system developed to penetrate the thick clouds of Venus in order to map that planet. Adams persuaded NASA to fly the system over the dense rain forest of Guatemala and found that the technique was just as effective in piercing the clouds and foliage of the jungle. When the radar images were analyzed, they indicated that the ancient Maya had developed an elaborate network of canals for irrigation, a much more advanced agricultural system than Morley and others had believed possible.

Over two million Indians of Maya descent live today in the area. Far from being a "vanished race," they are the second largest surviving indigenous American culture after the Quechua Indians of Peru and Bolivia. Like their ancestors, the contemporary Maya belong to various tribes. They speak related dialects that probably stem from a common language, but often one tribe cannot understand another's speech. The Yucatec of northern Yucatan number more than 350,000; the rest are divided into more than two dozen additional groups of various sizes, such as the Lacandon studied by Giles Healey.

Long contact with outside influences naturally have had an impact on modern Maya culture. Tourists on their way to the ruins pass through villages with Catholic churches, public schools where Spanish is taught to Mayan-speaking children, municipal buildings, shops, and sometimes movie theaters and gas stations. They catch glimpses from their bus windows of television sets and upholstered furniture alongside hammocks in thatched huts identical to those built by the ancient Maya.

But throughout the more than four centuries since the arrival of the Spanish, the Maya have managed to keep their identity. Many tribes still cling to ancient traditions. In the more remote villages these links with the past affect nearly every aspect of the present. Studying this "living archaeology" provides a valuable window into what life was like centuries ago.

In 1959, in a cave a few miles from Chichen Itza, a part-time guide discovered a passageway sealed with stones. Archaeologists and local Indians had investigated the Cave of Balankanche for years without finding anything. But now the amateur explorer broke through the wall of tightly cemented stones and crawled through a narrow chamber into a maze of tunnels. At the end was a large cavern containing dozens of pottery vessels and other objects. When the discovery was reported, a team of archaeologists, photographers, and artists went to work in the cave for five weeks. In spite of too much humidity and not enough oxygen, they recovered over six hundred artifacts. Some parts of the cave had been used as far back as 100 B.C.

The team had hardly begun work when a young Maya shaman, or native priest, came from a nearby village and explained that his

Figure of a Toltec-Itza warrior armed with spears. Temple of the Jaguars, Chichen Itza.
(*Drawing by Dolona Roberts*)

people had known for generations of a secret place of prayer dedicated to the rain god Tlaloc. But no one had been able to find this shrine to the Toltec counterpart of the Maya rain god Chac. When he saw the cavern, the shaman grew excited and asked permission to conduct special religious ceremonies there. He wanted to begin right away to placate Chac and the *balams*, guardians of the cave and the water sources. These scientists had invaded their sacred area, and they were sure to be displeased.

The ceremonies began the next morning and continued for twenty-four hours. The prayers and chanting droned on with occasional pauses for a drink of atole, the mixture of corn gruel and honey served in gourds. When the ceremony ended and the evil spirits had been swept out of the cave, the entrance was symbolically sealed for forty-eight hours. The exhausted celebrants feasted on a meal prepared by members of the shaman's village. There were chickens and turkeys wrapped in plantain leaves and baked in underground ovens and cakes of corn dough and spices, washed down with balche.

For perhaps a thousand years the cave had been all but forgotten, its existence preserved only in folklore. Yet the young shaman somehow knew how his ancestors would have revered that shrine centuries ago, using rituals he described as "intended for use in chambers hidden beyond the memory of man." In spite of the efforts of missionaries to replace pagan beliefs with Christian faith, the Maya continue to mix the two, maintaining a strong emphasis on magic, witchcraft, and superstition.

The modern Maya stands with one foot in the ancient world, one in the modern. He begs the favor of his ancestral gods before he plants his milpa—and attends mass on Sunday. She takes her new baby to church to be baptized—and then arranges the hetzmek. Meanwhile scientist-scholars will continue to explore the ruined cities until the secrets of the lost civilization are revealed and the mysteries of the ancient Maya are solved.

# GLOSSARY

*(Pronunciation guide to places, names and foreign phrases)*

Ah Puch (ah PUSH)—god of death

*Ahuacan* (ah-wah-KAHN)—highest class in Maya priesthood

Almehenob (ahl-MEH-heh-nahb)—Maya nobility

*Atole* (ah-TOH-lay)—thick, sweet drink made of *zacan*

*Bacabs* (BAH-kahbz)—important classification of gods

*Baktun* (BAHK-toohn)—unit of time in Maya calendar

Balankanche (bahl-ahn-kahn-CHAY)—cave near Chichen Itza where ancient rituals were practiced

*Balche* (bahl-CHAY)—kind of tree; used in making drink of fermented maize

*Batabs* (BAH-tahbs)—minor Maya chieftains

Belize City (bay-LEES)—former capital of Belize (British Honduras)

Bonampak (boh-nahm-PAHK)—ancient city in Chiapas, Mexico

Campeche (kam-PAY-chay)—state in Mexico on Yucatan Peninsula

*Cenote* (seh-NOH-tay)—caved-in limestone well

*Chac* (CHAHK)—important rain god; priest assisting at sacrifices and other ceremonies

Chiapas (chih-AHP-uhs)—state in Mexico on Pacific Ocean

Chichen Itza (chih-chen its-AH)—ancient city in Yucatan

*Chicleros* (chick-LEHR-ohs)—gatherers of *chicle*, juice used to make chewing gum

*Chilam Balam* (CHILL-um BAL-um)—collection of manuscripts written in Spanish by Indians of Yucatan

Chilan (chih-LAHN)—prophet who assisted priests

*Chultun* (choohl-TOON)—pit for storing water

*Codex/codices* (KOH-dehks; KAHD-ih-seez)—early book or manuscript

*Conquistador* (kahn-KEES-tuh-dohr)—Spanish conqueror

Copal (koh-PAHL)—kind of tropical tree yields resin called *pom*

Copan (koh-PAHN)—ancient city in western Honduras

Cozumel (kahz-ooh-MEHL)—island off the east coast of Yucatan

*Ex* (ESH)—loincloth worn by Maya men

Glyph (GLIHF)—symbol used in hieroglyphics

*Haab* (HAHB)—365-day civil year of Maya calendar

*Halac Uinic* (HAH-luhk ooh-EE-nihk)—"true man," supreme ruler of the Maya

Henequen (HEHN-eh-kehn)—plant raised for fiber; used in making rope

*Hetzmek* (HETS-mehk)—ceremony when baby is carried on the hip for the first time

Hieroglyphics (HI-roh-GLIHF-iks)—picture writing

*Huipil* (hwih-PEEL)—dress worn by Maya women

Hunab Ku (HOO-nab KOOH)—supreme being; creator of the Maya universe

Huanac Ceel (HWAH-nahk SIHL)—powerful thirteenth century ruler of Mayapan

Itza (its-AH)—Indian group that invaded Yucatan

Itzamna (its-ahm-NAH)—most important Maya god

Ix Chel (ISH CHEHL)—moon goddess, wife of Itzamna

Kabah (kah-BAH)—ancient city in Yucatan

*Katun* (KAT-oohn)—unit of time in Maya calendar

*Kin* (KIHN)—one day in Maya calendar

Kukulcan (koo-kuhl-KAHN)—Maya name for Quetzalcoatl

Labna (lahb-NAH)—ancient city in Yucatan

Lacandon (lah-kahn-DOHN)—Maya tribe living in Chiapas, Mexico

Mayapan (my-yuh-PAHN)—ancient city in Yucatan

Merida (MEHR-ih-duh)—major city in Yucatan

*Metate* (meh-TAH-tay)—stone for grinding maize

*Milpa* (MIHL-pah)—cornfield; system of agriculture

*Nacom* (NAH-kahm)—executioner at human sacrifices

Palenque (pah-LEHNK-ay)—ancient city in Chiapas, Mexico

*Pati* (PAH-tee)—cape worn by Maya men

Peten (peh-TEHN)—northern panhandle of Guatemala

Piedras Negras (pee-AY-druhs NAY-gruhs)—ancient city in Guatemala

*Pok-a-tok* (POHK-uh-tohk)—ball game played throughout Maya realm

*Pom* (PAHM)—resin of copal tree burned as incense

*Popul Vuh* (POH-puhl VOOH)—manuscript from Guatemala by Quiche-speaking Maya

*Pozole* (poh-SOH-lay)—drink made of *zacan* mixed with water

Quetzal (KEHTS-ahl)—brilliantly plumaged bird from Guatemalan highlands

Quetzalcoatl (KEHTS-ahl-KWAHT-uhl)—feathered serpent; legendary god-king

Quiche (kee-SHAY)—Maya tribe of Guatemala

*Rebozo* (ray-BOH-so)—shawl worn by Maya women

Rio Azul (REE-oh ah-SOOL)—site of ancient city in Guatemala

*Sacbe, sacbeob* (SAHK-bay, SAHK-bay-ahb)—"white roads" connecting city centers with outlying districts

Sayil (sah-EEL)—ancient city in Yucatan

Shaman (SHAY-muhn)—priest specializing in prayers and cures

Stela, stelae (STEE-lah, STEE-lie)—stone monument carved with dates

Tenochtitlan (teh-NOHSH-tiht-LAHN)—ancient Aztec capital

Tikal (tee-KAHL)—ancient city in Guatemala

Tlaloc (TLAH-luhk)—Toltec counterpart of Maya rain god Chac

Tollan (toh-LAHN)—ancient Toltec capital

Toltecs (TOHL-teks)—Indian conquerors of Maya in Yucatan

*Tortillas* (tohr-TEE-ahz)—thin, flat cakes made of ground corn

Tula (TOOH-lah)—town near Mexico City; site of ancient city of Tollan

Tulum (tooh-LOOHM)—ancient city in Quintana Roo, Mexico

*Tun* (TOOHN)—unit of Maya calendar

*Tzolkin* (TSOHL-kin)—160-day sacred year of Maya calendar

Uaxactun (wah-shahk-TOOHN)—ancient city in Guatemala

*Uinal* (ooh-EE-nuhl)—unit of Maya calendar

Uxmal (oosh-MAHL)—ancient city in Yucatan

*Yalba Uinicob* (YAHL-buh ooh-EEN-ih-kahb)—"lesser men," peasants

Yaxchilan (yahsh-chee-LAHN)—ancient city in Guatemala

Yucatan (yooh-kuh-TAHN)—peninsula in Gulf of Mexico; a state in Mexico

*Zacan* (ZAH-kahn)—dough made of ground corn

# INDEX